Say it in
Danish

BY
GERDA M. ANDERSEN

AND
THE EDITORIAL STAFF OF
DOVER PUBLICATIONS, INC.

D0816308

NEW YORK
DOVER PUBLICATIONS, INC.

Published in Canada by General Publishing Company, Ltd., 30 Lesmill Road, Don Mills, Toronto,
Ontario.
Published in the United Kingdom by Constable
and Company, Ltd., 10 Orange Street, London WC 2.

Standard Book Number: 486-20818-4
Library of Congress Catalog Card Number: 58-4228

Manufactured in the United States of America
Dover Publications, Inc.
180 Varick Street
New York, N.Y. 10014

CONTENTS

INTRODUCTION

SAY IT IN DANISH makes available to you, in simple usable form, most of the words and sentences you need for travel and everyday living in Denmark. The given English phrases are those shown by experience to be the most helpful. The translations are idiomatic rather than literal, for your primary goal is to make yourself understood. The Danish pronunciation is transcribed for you in the simple phonetic system explained below.

SENTENCE STRUCTURE

No attempt is made in this book to teach Danish grammar. Almost every given phrase and sentence is complete in itself and can be used without a knowledge of grammar.

The framework is designed to help you form additional sentences of your own. Thus, for the words in square brackets you can substitute the words immediately following (in the sentence or in the indented entries below). For example, the entry

> I am [hungry] thirsty.

provides two sentences: "I am hungry" and "I am thirsty." Three sentences are provided by the entry

> I am [a student].
> —— a teacher.
> —— a business man.

As your Danish vocabulary increases, you will find that you can form a wide range of phrases by substituting the proper words in these type-sentences.

Parentheses are used in this book for two purposes:
(1) To indicate an alternative phrase by words that may or may not be wanted in a sentence; example

I (do not) understand.

(2) To enclose explanatory matter; example
"*en smørrebrødsseddel*"
(a list of open-faced sandwiches).

Do not be deterred from speaking Danish by the fact that you will undoubtedly make grammatical errors. A native listener will usually grasp what you mean to say. However, you can avoid some errors by paying due attention to the gender of the nouns.

Danish uses two genders: *common* (*en*) and *neuter* (*et*); the indefinite articles. For your guidance, living beings: people, animals, fish, birds, insects, etc., are *mostly en*. As to the gender of objects, there is no rule; they may be either *et* or *en*.

Definite articles are suffixed to the noun. They are *en* for common gender nouns, *et* for neuter nouns and *ne* or *ene* for plural nouns.

Stolen—the chair
Stolene—the chairs
Børn—children
Børnene—the children

In lists of common objects, dishes, etc., genders are indicated by the use of the definite or indefinite articles.

THE INDEX

You will find the extensive index at the end of this book especially helpful. Capitalized items in the index refer to section headings; references to these main sections labeled "p." refer you to the page number. All other numbers in the index refer you to specific entry numbers and they are numbered consecutively from 1 up.

The primary purpose of the index is, of course, to enable you to locate quickly the specific word or phrase you need at the moment. But it can do more for you. If you will compare the various passages in which the same root-word occurs, you will discover a great deal about its grammatical inflection. You will also discover synonyms, idioms, and other related words.

PRONUNCIATION

SAY IT IN DANISH follows the official spelling, according to a revised system introduced in Denmark by law in 1948. This is the spelling visitors are likely to see in public notices, signs, and newspapers.

The simplified phonetic transcription is given as an aid to correct pronunciation of "Rigsdansk" (the acknowledged "high Danish"), omitting the various dialects spoken in Denmark. The transcription should be read as though it were English. Stressed syllables are printed in capital letters. In the phonetic system, consistency is sometimes sacrificed for simplicity and ease of comprehension. You are urged to use it only as a temporary guide. If you study Danish in a class or with a private teacher, you may be asked to omit it in order to avoid confusion with the accepted scientific phonetic system. Like English, Danish spelling and pronunciation are extremely irregular. This system does not attempt to initiate you into all the intricacies of Danish pronunciation but if you will follow the directions outlined below, you should be understood.

Danish vowels consist of one sound only, and are not

drawled. Consonants are often blurred. A peculiarity of the language is the glottal stop which has the effect of cutting off a word in the middle or at the end. It results in an abrupt utterance, followed by a slight sigh.

SCHEME OF PRONUNCIATION

Phonetic Transcription	Pronunciation	Notes
ă	as in cat	
ah	as in father	
ai	as in hair	
aw	as in hawk	
ĕ	like i in pit	
e, eh	as in met	
ee	as in feed	
ẽr	as in her	No exact equivalent in English. Round the lips as if to say oh but say eh. If you say girl, err, purr without pronouncing the r (as is done in England and some parts of the U.S.) you will give a good approximation. (This same sound occurs in German können, where it is short, and Goethe, where it is long.)

Phonetic Transcription	Pronunciation	Notes
ew	as in *few*	No exact equivalent in English. Round the lips as if to say *oo* but say *ee*. Practice by first saying *oo*, and WITHOUT CHANGING THE POSITION OF THE LIPS, say *ee*. (This sound is the same as the German *ü*, as in *müde*.)
ī	as in *bite*	
o	as in *awe*	
oh	as in *note*	This is a pure vowel, not a diphthong as in English. Practice by prolonging the sound *o* without permitting yourself to end on *oo*.
oo	as in *boot*	
ŏŏ	as in *foot*	
ow	as in *now*	
uh	as in the *boy*	
b	as in *bat*	
d	as in *day*	
f	as in *fat*	

Phonetic Transcription	Pronunciation	Notes
g	as in *girl*	Always pronounced hard, except in certain words where it is transcribed as *w*, but the exact Danish sound is almost impossible to indicate.
h	as in *hat*	
k	as in *kite*	Always a voiced sound as *k-nee* and never silent as in the English knife.
l	as in *veal*	
m	as in *man*	
n	as in *not*	
p	as in *pig*	
r	as in *more*	This sound is never rolled.
s	as in *simple*	
t	as in *time*	
th	as in *this*	This sound is between the voiced and unvoiced *th*.
v	as in *vat*	

Phonetic Transcription	Pronunciation	Notes
/	glottal stop	This represents the sudden cutting off of a voiced sound. Pronounced quickly as in *bottle* omitting *tt*.

THE DANISH ALPHABET

Å	å	aw
A	a	ă
B	b	bé
C	c	sé
D	d	dé
E	e	e
F	f	ef
G	g	gé (always hard)
H	h	haw/
I	i	ee
J	j	yawth
K	k	kaw/
L	l	l (very thin)
M	m	em
N	n	en
O	o	o/
P	p	pé
Q	q	not used
R	r	ehr
S	s	es
T	t	té
U	u	ŏŏ
V	v	vé
W	w	vé
X	x	x
Y	y	ew
Z	z	set
Æ	æ	(Ae combined in one letter)
Ø	ø	(Oe combined in one letter)

$$\frac{eh}{er}$$

GENERAL EXPRESSIONS
ALMINDELIGE UDTRYK

1. Yes.
Ja.
yă.

2. No.
Nej.
nĭ.

3. Perhaps.
Måske.
mo-SKÉ.

4. Excuse me.
Undskyld.
ohn-skewl'.

5. (Many) thanks.
(Mange) tak.
(mahng-eh) tăk.

6. You are welcome.
Åh, jeg be'r.   (Ikke noget at takke for.)
aw, yĭ bér.   (Ig-eh no-eth aw tak-keh for.)

7. It is all right.
Det er udmærket.
dé ehr OOTH-mehr-keth.

8. It is not all right.
Nej, det går ikke.
nĭ, dé gawr ig-eh.

9. That is all.
Det er alt.
dé ehr ahlt.

10. Wait a moment.
Vent et øjeblik.
Vent et OY-eh-blick.

11. Come in.
Kom ind.
kom in/.

12. Come here.
Kom her.
kom hehr.

13. What do you wish?
Hvad ønsker De?
vă ēīn-sker dee?

14. What?
Hvad?
văth? (vă?)

15. Who?
Hvem?
vem?

16. When?
Hvornår?
vor-NAWR?

17. Where?
Hvor?
vóhr/?

18. Why?
Hvorfor?
vor-for?

19. How long?
Hvor længe?
vor leng-eh?

20. How far?
Hvor langt?
vor lahnkt?

21. Listen here!
Hør her!
herr hehr!

22. Look out!
Pas på!
päs PAW/!

YOURSELF
DE SELV

23. I am an American citizen.
Jeg er amerikansk borger.
yĭ ehr ă-mé-ree-KÄNSK BOR-wer.

24. My name is John Smith.
Mit navn er John Smith.
meet nown/ ehr John Smith.

25. I spell my name ——.
Jeg staver mit navn ——.
yĭ stä-ver meet nown/ ——.

26. I am [a student].
Jeg er [student].
yĭ ehr [stŏŏ-DENT].

27. —— a teacher.
lærer.
LEH-rer.

28. —— a businessman.
forretningsmand.
for-RET-nings-män/.

29. I am here on [a business trip].
Jeg er her på [forretningsrejse].
yĭ ehr hehr paw [for-RET-nings-rĭ-seh].

30. —— **a vacation.**
   ferie.
   FÉR-yeh.

31. I am a friend of ——.
   Jeg er en ven af ——.
   yĭ ehr en ven/ ă ——.

32. My mailing address is ——.
   Min postadresse er ——.
   meen PAWST-ă-dres-seh ehr ——.

33. I am [hungry] thirsty.
   Jeg er [sulten] tørstig.
   yĭ ehr [SOOLT/n] TĒRRS-dee.

34. I am warm.
   Jeg er varm.
   yĭ ehr vahrm/.

35. I am cold.
   Jeg fryser.
   yĭ FREW-ser.

36. I am busy.
   Jeg har travlt.
   yĭ hahr trowlt/.

37. I am tired.
   Jeg er træt.
   yĭ ehr tret/.

38. I am ready.
   Jeg er færdig.
   yĭ ehr FEHR-dee.

39. I am glad.
   Det glæder mig.
   dé gleh-ther mĭ.

40. I am sorry.
   Det gør mig ondt.
   dé gĕrr mĭ ohnt/.

GREETINGS AND SOCIAL CONVERSATION

HILSEFORMER OG KONVERSATION

41. Good morning.
God morgen.·
go-MORN.

42. Good evening.
God aften.
go-ÄFT/n.

43. Good night.
God nat.
go-NÄT.

44. Good-bye.
Farvel.
far-VEL.

45. So long.
Farvel så længe.
far-VEL saw leng-eh.

46. Until the next time.
På gensyn.
paw GEN-sewn.

47. How are you?
Hvordan har De det?
VOH-den hahr dee dé?

48. Fine, thanks, and you?
Tak, godt; og De?
täk, got; aw dee?

49. How is your family?
Hvordan har familien det?
VOH-den hahr fä-MEEL-yen dé?

50. (Not) very well.
(Ikke så) godt.
(ig-eh saw) got.

51. How are things?
Hvordan står det til?
VOH-den stawr dé tél?

52. Very well, thanks.
Tak, udmærket.
tăk, OOTH-mehr-keth.

53. Not very well.
Ikke videre godt.
ig-eh vee-the-reh got.

54. May I introduce [Mr., Mrs.] Miss ——?
Må jeg præsentere [Hr., Fru] Frøken ——?
maw yĭ pré-sen-TÉ-reh [hehr, froo] frȳrk/n ——?

55. This is [my wife].
Det er [min kone].
dé ehr [meen KOH-neh].

56. —— my husband.
min mand.
meen măn/.

57. —— my daughter.
min datter.
meen dăd-der.

58. —— my son.
min søn.
meen sērn/.

59. —— my sister.
min søster.
meen sērst/r.

60. —— my brother.
min broder.
meen brohr.

61. —— my mother.
min moder.
meen mohr.

62. —— my father.
min fader.
meen far.

63. —— my child.
mit barn.
meet bar/n.

64. —— my friend (*masc.*)
min ven.
meen ven/.

65. —— my friend (*fem.*).
min veninde.
meen ven-IN-neh.

66. I am glad to meet you.
Det glæder mig at træffe Dem.
dé gleh-ther mĭ aw TREF-feh dem.

67. May I ask your name?
Må jeg spørge om Deres navn?
maw yĭ spĕrr-reh om deh-res nown?

68. Please sit down.
Værsgod og sid ned.
vehrs-go aw sith neth.

69. Who is [that boy]?
Hvem er [den dreng]?
vem ehr [den dreng/]?

70. —— that young man.
den unge mand.
den ohng-eh măn/.

71. —— that man (gentleman).
den mand (herre).
den măn/ (hehr-reh).

72. —— that woman (lady).
den kvinde (dame).
den kvin-neh (DĂ-meh).

73. May I have your address and telephone number?
Må jeg få Deres adresse og telefonnummer?
maw yĭ faw deh-res ă-DRES-seh aw té-lé-FOHN-nohm/r?

74. May I visit you again?
Må jeg besøge Dem igen?
maw yĭ bé-SĒR-weh dem ee-GEN?

75. Come and see us.
Kom og besøg os.
kom aw bé-SĒR os.

76. I have had a lovely time.
Det var vældig hyggeligt.
dé văr vel-dee hewg-geh-leet.

77. I have enjoyed myself very much.
Jeg har moret mig storartet.
yĭ hahr MOH-reth mĭ STOHR-ahr-teth.

78. Regards to your aunt and uncle.
Hils Deres tante og onkel.
heels/ deh-res TĂN-teh aw OHNK/l.

79. I like you very much.
Jeg synes så godt om Dem.
yĭ sewn/s saw got om dem.

80. I love you.
Jeg elsker dig.
yĭ EL-sker dĭ.

MAKING YOURSELF UNDERSTOOD
GØRE SIG FORSTÅELIG

81. Do you speak English?
Taler De engelsk?
tă-ler dee EHNG-elsk?

82. Does anyone here speak English?
Er der nogen her, der taler engelsk?
ehr dehr nohn hehr, dehr tă-ler EHNG-elsk?

83. I speak only English.
Jeg taler kun engelsk.
yĭ tă-ler kohn/ EHNG-elsk.

84. I know a little [Spanish].
Jeg kan lidt [spansk].
yĭ kăn lit [spăn/sk].

85. —— French.
fransk.
frăn/sk.

86. —— Italian.
italiensk.
ee-tăl-YEN/sk.

87. —— German.
tysk.
tewsk.

88. Please speak [slowly] more slowly.
Vær så venlig at tale [langsomt] langsommere.
vehr saw ven-lee aw tă-leh [LAHNG-somt] LAHNG-som·reh.

89. I (do not) understand.
Jeg forstår Dem (ikke).
yĭ for-STAWR/ dem (ig-eh).

90. Can you understand me?
Kan De forstå mig?
kăn dee for-STAW mĭ?

91. I (do not) know.
Jeg ved det (ikke).
yĭ vé dé (ig-eh).

92. I (do not) think so.
Jeg tror det (ikke).
yĭ trohr/ dé (ig-eh).

93. Please repeat it.
Vær så venlig at gentage det.
vehr saw ven-lee aw GEN-tä dé.

94. Please write it down.
Vær så venlig at skrive det ned.
vehr saw ven-lee aw skree-veh dé NÉTH.

95. What is that?
Hvad er det?
vă ehr dé?

96. What does that word mean?
Hvad betyder det ord?
vă bé-TEW-ther dé OH/r?

97. How do you say —— in Danish?
Hvad hedder —— på dansk?
vă HITH/r —— paw dăn/sk?

98. We need an interpreter.
Vi må have en tolk.
vee maw hă en TAWLK.

DIFFICULTIES
SMÅ PROBLEMER

99. Where is [the American Consulate]?
Hvor er [det amerikanske Konsulat]?
vohr ehr [dé ă-mé-ree-KĂN/-skeh kon-sŏŏ-LĂT]?

100. —— the police station.
politistationen.
po-lee-TEE-stă-SHO-nen.

101. —— the lost and found office.
Kontoret for fundne Sager.
kohn-TOH-reth for FOHN-neh SĂ-wer.

102. —— the washroom.
toilettet.
toh-ă-LET-eth.

103. —— the men's room.
herretoilettet.
HEHR-reh-toh-ă-LET-eth.

104. —— the ladies' room.
dametoilettet.
DĂ-meh-toh-ă-LET-eth.

105. Can you [help me] tell me?
Kan De [hjælpe mig] sige mig det?
kăn dee [YEL-peh mĭ] SEE-eh mĭ dé?

106. I am looking for my friends.
Jeg ser efter mine venner.
yĭ SÉR ef-ter mee-neh VEN/r.

107. I cannot find my hotel.
Jeg kan ikke finde mit hotel.
yĭ kăn ig-eh fin-neh meet ho-TEL/.

108. I do not remember [the number] the street.
Jeg kan ikke huske [gadenummeret] gadens navn.
*yĭ kăn ig-eh HŌŌ-skeh [GĂ-the-nohm-reth] GĂ-thens
nown.*

109. I have lost [my purse] my wallet.
Jeg har mistet [min taske] min tegnebog.
yĭ hahr MIST-eth [meen TĂS-keh] meen TĪ-neh-baw.

110. It is (not) my fault.
Det er (ikke) min skyld.
dé ehr (ig-eh) meen skewl/.

111. I forgot [my money] my keys.
Jeg glemte [mine penge] mine nøgler.
yĭ GLEM-teh [mee-neh PENG-eh] mee-neh NOY-ler.

112. I have missed my train.
Jeg kom for sent til toget.
yĭ kom for SÉN/t té TAW-wet.

113. What am I to do?
Hvad skal jeg gøre?
Vă skă yĭ GĒR-reh?

114. Where are we going?
Hvor skal vi hen?
vohr skă vee HEN/?

115. Go away.
Gå Deres vej.
gaw/ deh-res VĪ.

116. I will call a policeman.
Jeg kalder på en politibetjent.
yĭ KĂL/r paw en po-lee-TEE-bét-yent.

117. My money has been stolen.
Mine penge er stjaalet.
mee-neh PENG-eh ehr STYAWL-leth.

118. Help!
    Hjælp!
    yelp|!

119. Fire!
    Brand!
    Brån|!

120. Stop thief!
    Stop tyven!
    stop TEW-ven!

TRAVEL: CUSTOMS
REJSE: TOLDEN

121. Where is the customs?
    Hvor er tolden?
    vohr ehr TOL|n?

122. Here is [my baggage].
    Her er [min bagage].
    hehr ehr [meen bă-GĂ-sheh].

123. —— my health certificate.
    min sundhedsattest (vakcinationsattest).
    meen SOHN-héths-ă-TEST (vak-see-nă-SHOHNS-ă-TEST).

124. —— my identification.
    mit identitetskort.
    meet ee-den-tee-TÉTS-kawrt.

125. —— my landing card.
    mit landgangskort.
    meet LĂN-găngs-kawrt.

126. —— my passport.
    mit pas.
    meet păs.

127. This [bag] valise contains gifts.
Denne [taske] håndkuffert indeholder gaver.
den-neh [TÄS-keh] HON-kohf-fert in-é-HOL/r GÄ-ver.

128. The five pieces to your [left] right are mine.
De fem stykker til [venstre] højre for Dem er mine.
dee fem/ stĕrk/r té [VENS-treh] HOY-reh for dem ehr mee-neh.

129. I cannot find all my baggage.
Jeg kan ikke finde al min bagage.
yĭ kăn ig-eh fin-neh ahl meen bă-GÄ-sheh.

130. I have [nothing] something to declare.
Jeg har [intet] noget at fortolde.
yĭ hahr [IN-tet] NOH-eth aw for-TOL-leh.

131. Must I open everything?
Er jeg nødt til at åbne det hele?
ehr yĭ nērt té aw AWB-neh dé hé-lé?

132. I cannot open the trunk.
Jeg kan ikke åbne den store kuffert.
yĭ kăn ig-eh AWB-neh den STOH-reh kohf-fert.

133. All this is for my personal use.
Alt dette er til mit personlige brug.
ahlt det-teh ehr té meet pehr-SOHN-lee-eh brŏŏ.

134. There is nothing here but clothing.
Der er intet andet her end klæder.
Dehr ehr in-tet ăn-neth hehr in klehr.

135. Are these things dutiable?
Er disse ting toldpligtige?
ehr dees-seh ting/ TOL-plék-tee-eh?

136. That is all I have.
Det er alt, hvad jeg har.
dé ehr ahlt vă yĭ hahr.

137. How much must I pay?

Hvor meget skal jeg betale?

vor mĭ-eth skă yĭ bé-TĂ-leh?

138. Have you finished?

Er De færdig?

ehr dee FEHR-dee?

BAGGAGE
BAGAGE

139. The parcel check room.

Garderoben.

gahr-dé-ROH-ben.

140. I want to leave these bags here for a few days.

Jeg vil gerne lade disse kufferter stå et par dage.

yĭ vé gehr-neh lă dees-seh kohf-fer-ter staw et pär DĂ-eh.

141. Where is the baggage checked?

Hvor indskrives bagagen?

vohr IN-skree-ves bă-GĂ-shen?

142. The baggage room.

Rejsegodsekspeditionen.

RĬ-seh-gohs-ex-pé-dee-SHOH-nen.

143. The baggage check.

Garantisedlen.

gă-răn-TEE-seth-len.

144. Can I check my baggage through to —— on this ticket?

Kan jeg indskrive min bagage til —— på denne billet?

kă yĭ IN-skree-veh meen bă-GĂ-sheh té —— paw den-neh bee-LET?

145. I wish to take out my baggage.

Jeg vil gerne have min bagage udleveret.

yĭ vé gehr-neh hä meen bă-GĂ-sheh OOTH-lé-vé-reth.

146. Where can I find a porter?

Hvor finder jeg en drager?

vohr FIN/r yĭ en DRAH-wer?

147. What is your number?

Hvad er Deres nummer?

vă ehr deh-res NOHM/r?

148. Follow me, please.

Følg bare mig.

FERL bah-reh mĭ.

149. Handle this carefully.

Tag forsigtigt på dette.

TĂ/ for-SIK-teet paw det-teh.

150. Put it all in a taxi.

Sæt det hele i en taxa.

Set dé hé-lé ee en taxă.

DIRECTIONS

OPLYSNINGER

151. Can you recommend a travel agency?

Kan De anbefale et rejsebureau?

kä dee ÄN-bé-fä-leh et RĬ-seh-bew-ro?

152. I want to go to [the airline office] the Danish tourist office.

Jeg skal hen til [luftfartskontoret] det danske Turistkontor.

yĭ skă hen/ té [LOHFT-fahrts-kohn-TOH-ret] dé DÄN-skeh tŏŏ-REEST-kohn-TOHR.

153. Is the bus stop near here?
Er bus-stoppestedet nær herved?
ehr BOOS-stop-peh-steh-thet nehr/ hehr-vé?

154. How long will it take to go to the airport?
Hvor lang tid tager det at komme ud til luft-havnen?
Vor lahng teeth tahr dé aw kom-meh ooth té LOHFT-how-nen?

155. When will we arrive at ——?
Hvornår ankommer vi til ——?
vor-NAWR AN-kom-mer vee té ——?

156. Is this the direct way to ——?
Er dette den nærmeste vej til ——?
ehr det-teh den nehr-mé-steh vī té ——?

157. Please show me the way [to the business section].
Vær så venlig at vise mig vejen [til forretnings-kvarteret].
Vehr saw ven-lee aw vee-seh mī vī-en [té for-RET-nings-kvar-té-ret].

158. —— to the department stores.
til stormagasinerne.
té STOHR-mă-gă-see-ner-neh.

159. Should I turn [to the east]?
Skal jeg dreje [mod øst]?
skă yī drī-eh [mohth ERST]?

160. —— to the west.
mod vest.
mohth VEST.

161. —— to the north.
mod nord.
mohth NOHR/.

162. —— to the south.
mod syd.
mohth SEWTH.

163. —— to the right.
til højre.
té HOY-reh.

164. —— to the left.
til venstre.
té VEN-streh.

165. —— at the traffic light.
ved lyskurven.
vé LEWS-kŏŏr-ven.

166. It is [on this side of the street], isn't it?
Det er [på denne side af gaden], ikke sandt?
Dé ehr [paw den-neh see-the ă GĂ-then], ig-eh SĂNT?

167. —— on the other side of the boulevard.
på den anden side af boulevarden.
paw den ĂN-nen see-the ă bŏŏ-leh-VAHR-den.

168. —— at the corner of the avenue.
på hjørnet af alléen.
paw YĔRR-neth ă Ă-lé-én.

169. —— across the bridge.
over broen.
ow/r BROH-ɛn.

170. —— inside the station.
inde på banegården.
in-neh paw BĂ-neh-gaw-ren.

171. —— outside the building.
udenfor bygningen.
oo-then-for BEWG-ning-en.

172. —— **opposite the city hall.**
overfor Rådhuset.
ow/r-for rawth-hoo-seth.

173. —— **beside the café.**
ved siden af kaféen.
vé see-then ă kă-FÉ-én.

174. —— **in front of the statue.**
foran statuen.
for-ăn STĂ-too-en.

175. —— **behind the school.**
bagved skolen.
bă-vé SKOH-len.

176. —— **straight ahead from the square.**
lige ud fra torvet.
LEE-eh ooth fră TOR-veth.

177. —— **in the middle of the circle.**
midt på runddelen.
mét paw ROHN/-dé-len.

178. **It is forward, isn't it?**
Det er fremefter, ikke sandt?
dé ehr FREM-ef-ter, ig-eh SĂNT?

179. —— **back.**
tilbage.
té-BĂ-weh.

180. —— **in this direction.**
i denne retning.
ee den-neh RET-ning.

181. —— **in that direction.**
i den der retning.
ee den DEHR RET-ning.

182. Is it near?
Er det nærved?
ehr dé NEHR/-véth?

183. How far is it?
Hvor langt væk er det?
vor lahngt vek ehr dé?

184. How does one go there?
Hvordan kommer man dertil?
vor-DĂN kom-mer măn dehr-TIL?

185. Can I walk there?
Kan jeg gå derhen?
kăn yĭ GAW/ dehr-hen?

186. Which is the fastest way?
Hvilken vej er hurtigst?
vil-ken vĭ ehr HŌŎR-teest?

187. Am I going in the right direction?
Går jeg i den rigtige retning?
gawr yĭ ee den rik-tee-eh RET-ning?

TICKETS
BILLETTER

188. Where is [the ticket office]?
Hvor er [billetkontoret]?
vohr ehr [bee-LET-kohn-toh-reth]?

189. —— the waiting room.
ventesalen.
VEN-teh-să-len.

190. —— the information bureau.
oplysningskontoret.
OP-lews-nings-kohn-toh-reth.

191. How much is a [one-way ticket] round trip to ——?

Hvad koster en [enkeltbillet] tur-retur til ——?

va kos-ter en [EN-kelt-bee-LET] too-ré-toor té ——?

192. I want [a ticket].

Jeg vil gerne have [en billet].

yĭ vé gehr-neh hä [en bee-LET].

193. —— a seat near the window.

en vinduesplads.

en VIN-dŏŏs-pläs.

194. —— a reserved seat.

en pladsbillet.

en PLÄS-bee-LET.

195. —— a ticket for the sleeper.

en sovevognsbillet.

en SOW-eh-vowns-bee-LET.

196. —— a compartment.

en hel kupé.

en hél/ kŏŏ-PÉ.

197. —— a timetable.

en køreplan.

en KĒR-reh-plä/n.

198. I want to go [first class].

Jeg kører [på første klasse].

yĭ kēr-rer [paw FĒRR-steh kläs-seh].

199. —— tourist class.

på fællesklasse.

paw FEL-les-kläs-seh.

200. Can I get something to eat on the trip?

Kan jeg få noget at spise undervejs?

kä yĭ faw noh-et aw SPEE-seh ohn-ner-vĭs?

201. May I stop at —— on the way?
Kan jeg gøre ophold i —— på vejen?
kä yĭ ger-reh OP-hol ee —— paw VI̠/-en?

202. Can I go by way of ——?
Kan jeg tage over ——?
kä yĭ tä ow/r ——?

203. How long is this ticket good?
Hvor længe gælder denne billet?
vor-leng-eh GEL/r den-neh bee-LET?

204. How much baggage may I take?
Hvor meget bagage må jeg have med?
vor mĭ-eth bă-GÄ-sheh maw yĭ hă meth?

AIRPLANE
FLYVEMASKINE

205. Is there bus service to the airport?
Er der bus service til lufthavnen?
ehr dehr bŏŏs "service" té LOHFT-how-nen?

206. At what time must I be at the place of departure?
Hvad tid skal jeg være på afgangsstedet?
vă teeth skä yĭ veh-reh paw OW-gahngs-steh-thet?

207. When is there a flight to ——?
Hvornår går der en flyvemaskine til ——?
vor-NAWR gawr dehr en FLEW-veh-mä-skee-neh té ——?

208. What is the flight number?
Hvad er flight nummeret?
vă ehr "flight" nohm/reth?

209. My ticket is ordered but not confirmed.
Min billet er bestilt, men ikke bekræftet.
meen bee-LET ehr bé-STILT, men ig-eh bé-kref-teth.

210. Are meals served on the plane?
Serveres der måltider i flyvemaskinen?
sehr-vé-res dehr MOL-tee-ther ee FLEW-veh-mă-skee-nen?

211. How many kilos may one take?
Hvor mange kilo må man have?
vor mahng-eh KEE-loh maw măn hă/?

212. How much per kilo for excess baggage?
Hvad koster det per kilo i overvægt?
vă kos-ter dé pehr KEE-loh ee OW/r-vekt?

BOAT
SKIB

213. Bon voyage!
God rejse!
GO/ rĭ-seh!

214. All aboard!
Alle passagerer ombord!
ăl-leh pă-să-SHEH-rer ŏm-BOHR!

215. Is it time to go on board?
Skal man gå ombord nu?
skă măn gaw om-BOHR NŎŎ?

216. Can I go by ferry to ——?
Kan jeg komme med færge til ——?
kă yĭ kom-meh meh FEHR-weh té ——?

217. When does the next boat leave?
Hvornår går det næste skib?
vor-NAWR gawr dé nes-teh skeeb?

218. Can I land at ——?
Kan jeg gå i land i ——?
kä yĭ gaw ee-LAN/ ee ——?

219. Will you [prepare my berth]?
Vil De [gøre min køje i stand]?
vé dee [gēr-reh meen KOY-eh] ee-stän/?

220. —— open the porthole.
åbne koøjet.
awb-neh KOH-oy-et.

221. —— open the ventilator.
lukke op for ventilatoren.
lohk-keh op for ven-tee-LA-torn.

222. I want to rent a deck chair.
Jeg vil gerne leje en liggestol.
yĭ vé gehr-neh lĭ-yeh en lig-geh-stohl.

223. Where do I find [the purser]?
Hvor finder jeg [regnskabsføreren]?
vohr FIN/r yĭ [RĬN-skäbs-fēr-ren]?

224. —— the steward.
hovmesteren.
HOW-mes-tren.

225. —— the cabin steward.
kahyts-stewarden.
kä-HEWTS-steward/in.

226. —— the stewardess.
stewardessen.
stewar-DES-sen.

227. —— the captain.
kaptajnen.
käp-TĬ/-nen.

228. I am going [to my cabin].
Jeg går [ned i min kahyt].
y̆l gawr [néth ee meen kă-HEWT].

229. —— to the upper deck.
op på øverste dæk.
op paw ER͞-vehr-steh deck.

230. —— to the lower deck.
ned på nederste dæk.
néth paw NÉ-ther-steh deck.

231. —— to the dock (to the pier).
ned i dokken (ned på kajen).
néth ee DOCK/n (néth paw KĪ/-en).

232. I am going to be seasick.
Jeg er ved at blive søsyg.
y̆l ehr vé aw blee-eh SER͞-sewh.

233. Do you have any seasick tablets?
Har De nogen søsygetabletter?
hahr dee nohn SER͞-sewh-eh-tă-BLET/r?

234. The lifeboat.
Redningsbåden.
RETH-nings-baw-then.

235. The life preserver.
Redningsbæltet.
RETH-nings-bel-teth.

TRAIN
TOG

236. The arrival.
Ankomsten.
ĂN-koms-ten.

237. The departure.
Afgangen.
OW-gahng-en.

238. Where is the Central Station?
Hvor er Hovedbanegården?
vohr ehr HOH-eth-bă-neh-GAWR/n?

239. —— the Eastern Railway Station.
Østbanegården.
$\overline{ERST}$-bă-neh-GAWR/n.

240. When does [the train] for —— leave?
Hvornår går [toget] til ——?
vor-NAWR GAWR [taw-wet] té ——?

241. Is the train from —— [late] on time?
Er toget fra —— [forsinket] rettidigt?
ehr taw-wet frå —— [for-SIN-geth] RET-tee-theet?

242. My train leaves in ten minutes.
Mit tog går om ti minutter.
meet TAWH GAWR/ om tee mee-NŎŎD/r.

243. From [what platform] what track does the train leave?
Fra [hvilken perron] hvilket spor går toget?
frå [vil-ken peh-RONG] vil-ket SPOHR GAWR taw-wet?

244. Does the train stop at ——?
Standser toget i ——?
STĂN-ser taw-wet ee ——?

245. How long does the train stop at ——?
Hvor længe holder toget i ——?
vor LENG-eh HOL/r taw-wet ee ——?

246. Can I get [an express] a local to ——?
Kan jeg få [et eksprestog] et bumletog til ——?
kă yĭ faw [et ex-PRESS-taw] et BOHM/-leh-taw té ——?

247. Is there [a later] an earlier train?
Er der [et senere] et tidligere tog?
ehr dehr [et SÉ-né-reh] et TEETH-lee-reh tawh?

248. Please [open] close the window.
Vær så venlig at [åbne] lukke vinduet.
vehr saw ven-lee aw [AWB-neh] LOHG-geh vin-dŏŏ-eth.

249. Where is [the dining car]?
Hvor er [spisevognen]?
vohr ehr [SPEE-seh-vow-nen]?

250. —— the smoking car.
rygevognen.
REW-eh-vow-nen.

251. —— the sleeper.
sovevognen.
SOW-eh-vow-nen.

252. —— the baggage car.
rejsegodsvognen.
RĪ-seh-gohs-vow-nen.

253. Is this seat taken?
Er denne plads optaget?
ehr den-neh plås OP-tă-eth?

254. Do you mind if I smoke?
Tillader De, at jeg ryger?
TÉ-lă-ther dee, ă yī REW-ehr?

BUS, STREETCAR AND SUBWAY
BUS, SPORVOGN OG S-TOG

255. What [bus] streetcar, subway do I take to go to ——?

Hvad for [en bus] sporvogn, et S-tog skal jeg tage for at komme til ——?

vă-for [en bōōs] SPOHR-vown, et S-tawh skă yĭ tă for aw kom-meh té ——?

256. How much is [the fare] a transfer?

Hvad koster [billetten] en omstigningsbillet?

vă kos-ter [bee-LET/n] en OM-steeg-nings-bee-LET?

257. Driver, do you go near ——?

Konduktør, kommer De i nærheden af ——?

kon-dōōk-TERR, kom-mer dee ee nehr-hé-then ă ——?

258. Will I have to change?

Skal jeg stige om?

skă yĭ stee-eh OM/?

259. Please tell me where to get off.

Vær venlig og sig mig, hvor jeg skal stå af.

vehr ven-lee aw SEE/ mĭ, VOHR yĭ skă staw ă/.

260. I want to get off at the next stop.

Jeg vil gerne af ved næste stoppested.

yĭ vé gehr-neh Ă/ vé neh-steh STOP-peh-steth.

261. The interurban bus.

Rutebilen.

ROOT-eh-bee-len.

TAXI
TAXA (BIL)

262. Will you call a taxi for me.
Vil De skaffe mig en taxa.
vé dee skǻf-feh mĭ en taxa.

263. Are you free?
Er De ledig?
ehr dee LÉ-thee?

264. What do you charge per [hour] kilometer?
Hvad tager De pr. [time] kilometer?
vǻ tahr dee pehr [TEE-meh] kee-loh-MÉ-ter?

265. How much will the ride cost?
Hvor meget kommer turen til at koste?
vor-MĬ-eth kom-mer TOO-ren té ä kos-teh?

266. I would like to drive around the city for an hour.
Jeg vil gerne køre en tur gennem byen på en time.
yĭ vé gehr-neh KĒR-reh en toor gen-nem BEW-en paw en TEE-meh.

267. Please drive [more slowly] more carefully.
Vær så venlig at køre [langsommere] mere forsigtigt.
vehr saw ven-lee aw KĒR-reh [LAHNG-som/reh] mé-reh for-SIK-teet.

268. Can you stop here?
Kan De holde her?
kä dee HOL-leh hehr?

269. Will you wait for me?
Vil De vente på mig?
vé dee VEN-teh paw mĭ?

AUTOMOBILE TRAVEL
MOTORKØRSEL; REJSE pr. BIL

270. Where can I rent [a car]?
Hvor kan jeg leje [en bil] ?
VOHR kă yĭ lĭ-eh [en BEEL]?

271. —— a motor cycle.
en motorcykel.
en MO-tor-seekl.

272. —— a motor scooter.
en motor scooter.
en "motor scooter."

273. I have an international driver's license.
Jeg har et internationalt kørekort.
yĭ hahr et IN-ter-nă-sho-nält KĒR-reh-kort.

274. What [town] is this?
Hvad er det for en [by]?
vă ehr dé for en [BEWĬ]?

275. —— village.
landsby.
LĂNS-bew.

276. —— city.   **277. —— suburb.**
storby.   forstad.
STOHR-bew.   *FOR-stäth.*

278. What is the next town?
Hvad hedder den næste by?
vă hither den neh-steh bew|?

279. Where does that road go?
Hvor fører den vej hen?
vohr fĕr-rer den vĭ hen?

280. Is the road [rough]?
Er vejen [ujævn]?
ehr vĭ/-en [OO-yevn]?

281. —— smooth.
jævn.
yevn.

282. —— paved.
asfalteret.
äs-fäl-TÉ-reth.

283. —— bad.
dårlig.
DAWR-lee.

284. —— good.
god.
GOH/.

285. Can you show it to me on the road map?
Kan De vise mig det på kortet?
kä dee VEE-seh mĭ dé paw KAWR-teth?

286. Where can I find a [gas station] garage?
Hvor finder jeg en [benzin-tank] garage?
vohr FIN/r yĭ en [ben-SEEN-tänk]? gä-RÄ-sheh?

287. The tank is [empty] full.
Tanken er [tom] fuld.
tänk/n ehr [tom/] fŏŏl/.

288. How much is gas per liter?
Hvad koster benzinen pr. liter?
vä kos-ter ben-SEE-nen pehr leet-ter?

289. Give me forty liters.
Giv mig fyrre liter.
gee mĭ FER-reh leet-ter.

290. Will you change the oil?
Vil De skifte olien?
vé dee skeef-teh OHL-yen?

291. [Light, medium] heavy oil.
[Tynd, mellemtyk] tyk olie.
[*tērn*/, *mel-lem-tewk*] *tewk OHL-yeh.*

292. Put water in the battery.
Kom vand på batteriet.
Kom vänn/ paw băt-eh-REE-eth.

293. Recharge the battery.
Lad batteriet op.
lăth băt-eh-REE-eth OP.

294. Lubricate the car.
Smør bilen.
smēr/r BEÉ-len.

295. Could you wash it [now] soon?
Kunde De vaske den [nu] om lidt?
kŏŏ dee văs-keh den [nŏŏ] om lit?

296. I would like to leave my car here for the night.
Jeg vil gerne lade min bil stå her i nat.
yĭ vé gehr-neh lă meen beel STAW hehr ee-NĂT.

297. Can you recommend a good mechanic?
Kan De anbefale en god mekaniker?
kăn dee ĂN-bé-fă-leh en GO/ mé-KĂ-nee-ker?

298. Will you adjust the brakes.
Vil De ordne bremsen.
vé dee ord-neh BREM-sen.

299. Check the tires.
Se dækkene efter.
sé DEK-keh-neh EFT/r.

300. Can you repair a puncture?
Kan De reparere en punktering?
kăn dee ré-pă-ré-ré en POHNG-té-ring?

301 The motor overheats.
Motoren bliver for varm.
mo-TOH-ren bleer for vahrm/.

302. The engine [misses] stalls.
Motoren [slår ud] staller.
mo-TOH-ren [slawr OOTH] STÅL/r.

303. There is [a grinding noise].
Der er [noget der skurrer].
dehr ehr [no-eth dehr SKOOR-rer].

304. —— a rattling noise.
noget der rasler.
no-eth dehr RÅS-ler.

305. —— a slow leak.
en lille utæthed.
en leel-leh OO-tet-héth.

306. May I park here for a few hours?
Må jeg parkere her et par timer?
maw yĭ par-KĒ-reh hehr et pår TEE-mer?

HELP ON THE ROAD
HJÆLP PÅ LANDEVEJEN

307. I am sorry to trouble you.
Undskyld jeg ulejliger Dem.
OHN-skewl yĭ ŏŏ-LĪ/-leer dem.

308. My car has broken down.
Min vogn har fået en skade.
meen vown hahr faw-eth en skå-the.

309. Will you help me get it off the road?
Vil De hjælpe mig med at få den væk fra kørebanen?
vé dee yel-peh mĭ meh aw faw den vek frä KĒR-reh-bänen?

310. Can you [push] tow the car?
Kan De [skubbe] trække vognen?
kän dee [skohb-beh] trek-keh vow-nen?

311. Can you help me change a tire?
Kan De hjælpe mig med at skifte dæk?
kän dee yel-peh mĭ meh aw skeef-teh dek?

312. May I borrow a jack?
Må jeg låne en donkraft?
Maw yĭ law-neh en DOHN-kräft?

313. My car is stuck in the mud.
Min vogn sidder fast i mudder.
meen vown sither fäst ee mōōth/-ther.

314. My car is stuck in the ditch.
Min vogn er kørt i grøften.
meen vown ehr kĕrrt ee GRĒRF-ten.

315. Could you give me a lift to a garage?
Kunde De køre mig hen til en garage?
kŏŏ dee kĕr-reh mĭ hen té en gä-RÄ-sheh?

PARTS OF THE CAR
BILDELE OG TILBEHØR

316. The accelerator.   Speederen.   *SPEE-deh-ren.* *
317. The battery.   Batteriet.   *bä-té-REE-eth.*

* In Danish the definite article is suffixed to the noun. Genders are
neuter (*et*) and common (*en*).

318. The bolt. Bolten. *BOL/ten.*

319. The brake. Bremsen. *BREM-sen.*

320. The clutch. Koblingen. *KOP-ling-en.*

321. The engine. Motoren. *mo-TOH-ren.*

322. The gear shift. Gearskiftet. *GEER-skeef-teth.*

323. The headlight. Forlygten. *FOR-lērk-ten.*

324. The horn. Bilhornet. *BEEL-hohrn-eth.*

325. The nut. Møtriken. *MĒR-tré-ken.*

326. The spark plug. Tændrøret. *TEN-rēr-ret.*

327. The spring. Fjederen. *FYÉ-ren.*

328. The starter. Selvstarteren. *SEL-star-té-ren.*

329. The steering wheel. Rattet. *RAHT-teth.*

330. The tail light. Baglygten. *BAHG-lērk-ten.*

331. The spare tire. Reservedækket. *ré-SEHR-veh-dek-eth.*

332. The spare wheel. Reservehjulet. *ré-SEHR-veh-yoo-leth.*

333. The windshield wiper. Vinduesviskeren.
VIN-dōōs-visk-eren.

TOOLS AND EQUIPMENT
REDSKABER OG UDSTYR

334. The chains. Kæderne. *KEH-ther-neh.*

335. The hammer. Hammeren. *HÄM-meh-ren.*

336. The jack. Donkraften. *DOHN-kräft/n.*

337. The pliers. Niptangen. *NIP-tahng-en.*

338. The rope. Rebet. *RÉ-beth.*

339. The screwdriver. Skruetrækkeren. *SKROO-eh-trek/ren.*

340. The tire pump. Luftpumpen. *LOHFT/-pohm-pen.*

341. The wrench. Skruenøglen. *SKROO-eh-noy-len.*

ROAD AND TRAFFIC SIGNS
VEJSKILTE: FÆRDSELTSTAVLER

This section has been alphabetized in Danish to facilitate the tourist's reading of Danish signs. For English alphabetization, please see index.

342. **Brug hornet.** Sound your horn. *Brŏŏ/ HOHR-neth.*

343. **Brug andet gear.** Use second gear. *Brŏŏ/ ăn-neth GEER.*

344. **Bugtet Vej.** Winding road.' *BOHK-teth vĭ/.*

345. **Dobbeltsving.** Double curve. *DOPL-SVING/.*

346. **Ensrettet Færdsel.** One Way. *ÉNS-ret-eth FEHR-sel.*

347. **Fald.** Dip. *făl/.*

348. **Gadekryds.** (Street) Intersection. *GĂ-the-krews.*

349. **Hold til [højre] venstre.** Keep [right] left. *HOL/ té [HOY-reh] VEN-streh.*

350. **Hospital.** Hospital. *HOH-spee-TĂL/.*

351. **Ingen Gennemkørsel.** No thoroughfare. *ING-en GEN-nem-kĕrr-sel.*

352. **Ingen Parkering.** No parking. *ING-en pahr-KÉ-ring.*

353. **Jernbaneoverskæring.** Railroad crossing. *YEHRN-bă-neh-OW/r-skeh-ring.*

354. **Kør.** Go. *kĕrr.*

355. **Kør forsigtigt.** Drive carefully. *kĕrr for-SIK-teet.*

356. **Korsvej.** Crossroads. *KORS-vĭ/.*

357. **Langsom kørsel.** Slow down. *LAHNG-som kĕrr-sel.*

358. **Maksimalhastighed —— kilometer.** Maximum speed —— kilometers. *max-ee-MĂL-hă-stee-héth —— kee-lo-MÉ-ter.*

359. **Omkørsel.** Detour. *OM-kĕrr-sel.*

360. **Parkering.** Parking. *păr-KÉ-ring.*

361. **Parkering Forbudt.** No Parking. *păr-KÉ-ring for-BŎŎT/.*

362. **Skarpt Sving.** Sharp turn. *skărpt sving/.*

363. **Skole.** School. *SKOH-leh.*

364. **Smal Vej.** Narrow road. *smăl vĭ/.*

365. **Stejl Bakke.** Steep grade. *stĭl/ BĂK-keh.*

366. **Stop.** Stop. *stop.*

367. Sving. Curve. *sving|.*

368. Udsving til [højre] venstre forbudt.
No [right] left turn.
OOTH-sving| té [HOY-reh] VEN-streh for-BŎOT|.

369. Vejarbejde. Road repairs. *VĪ-är-bī-deh.*

370. Vejskæring. (Road) Intersection. *VĪ-skeh-ring.*

PUBLIC NOTICES
OFFENTLIGE OPSLAG

371. Åben. Open. *AW-ben.*

372. Adgang forbudt. No admittance. *ÄTH-gahng for-BŎOT|.*

373. Fare. Danger. *FAH-reh.*

374. Indgang. Entrance. *IN-gahng.*

375. Kom ind. Come in. *kom IN|.*

376. Ledig. Vacant. *LÉ-thee.*

377. Lukket. Closed. *LOHG-geth.*

378. Man bedes ——. You are requested to ——.
man BÉ-thes ——.

379. Optaget. Occupied. *OP-tä-eth.*

380. Publikum anmodes om ——.
The public is requested to ——.
pŏŏb-lee-kŏŏm ÄN-moh-thes om ——.

381. Ring. Ring. *ring|.*

382. Spytning forbudt. No Spitting. *spē̆rt-ning for-BŎOT|.*

383. Til Leje. For rent. *té LI-eh.*

384. Tobaksrygning forbudt. No Smoking.
toh-BĂKS-rew-ning for-BŎOT|.

385. Træk. Pull. *trek.*

386. Tryk. Push. *trē̆k.*

387. Udgang. Exit. *OOTH-gahng.*

COMMUNICATIONS: TELEPHONE
KOMMUNIKATIONSMIDLER: TELEFON

388. May I use your telephone?
Må jeg benytte Deres telefon?
maw yī bé-nēŕt-teh deh-res té-lé-FOHN?

389. Will you telephone for me?
Vil De telefonere for mig?
vé dee té-lé-foh-NÉ-reh for mī?

390. I would like to make a local call, number ——.
Jeg vil gerne ringe til et indenbys-nummer ——.
yī vé gehr-neh ring-eh té et IN-en-bews-nohm/r ——.

391. My number is ——.
Mit nummer er ——.
meet nohm/r ehr ——.

392. How much is a long-distance call to ——?
Hvad koster en udenbys samtale til ——?
vā kos-ter en ŌŌ-then-bews säm-tä-leh té ——?

393. The operator will call you. (lit. We'll ring you.)
Vi ringer!
vee RING-er!

394. The operator.
Telefondamen.
té-lé-FOHN-dä-men.

395. Hello, hello.
Hallo, hallo.
häl-loh, häl-loh.

396. They do not answer.
De svarer ikke.
dee svah-rer ig-eh.

397. There is no answer.
Der er ingen svar.
dehr ehr ING-en svahr.

398. The line is busy.
Der er optaget.
dehr ehr OP-tä-eth.

399. May I speak to the manager?
Må jeg tale med direktøren?
maw yī tä-leh meh dee-rek-TER-ren?

400. This is Mr. —— speaking. (lit. You're speaking with Mr. ——.)
De taler med Hr. ——.
dee tä-ler meh hehr/ ——.

401. One moment ——.
Et øjeblik ——.
et OY-eh-blik ——.

402. He is not in.
Han er ikke tilstede.
hän ehr ig-eh té-STEH-the.

403. Will you take a message?
Vil De tage imod en besked?
vé dee tä ee-mohth en bé-SKÉTH?

404. I will call back later.
Jeg ringer senere.
yī ring-er SÉ-né-reh. ——

405. There is a telephone call for you.
Der er telefon til Dem.
dehr ehr télé-FOHN té dem.

406. Good-bye.
 Farvel.
 făr-VEL.

POST OFFICE
POSTHUS

407. I am looking for [a post office].
 Jeg søger [et posthus].
 yĭ SĔR-wer [et PAWST-hoos].

408. —— a letter box.
  en brevkasse.
  en BRĔV-kăs-seh.

409. To which window should I go?
 Hvilket vindue skal jeg henvende mig ved?
 vél-keth VIN-dŏŏ skä yĭ HEN-ven-neh mĭ véth?

410. I want to send this [via airmail].
 Jeg ønsker at sende dette [pr. luftpost].
 yĭ ĕrn-sker aw sen-neh det-teh [pehr LOHFT-pawst].

411. —— regular mail.
  som almindelig brevpost.
  som ăl-MÉN-neh-lee BRÉV-pawst.

412. —— registered mail.
  anbefalet.
  ĂN-bé-fä-leth.

413. —— parcel post.
  som pakkepost.
  som PAHK-keh-pawst.

414. —— general delivery.
  poste restante.
  paws-teh ré-stahng-teh.

415. —— special delivery.
som ekspresbrev.
som ex-PRESS-brév.

416. —— air freight.
som luftpostpakke.
som LOHFT-pawst-pahk-keh.

417. I would like this package insured for ——.
Jeg vil gerne have denne pakke forsikret for ——.
yĭ vé gehr-neh hä den-neh pahk-keh for-SIK-reth for ——.

418. Will you give me six airmail stamps?
Vil De give mig seks luftpost-frimærker?
vé dee gee mĭ sex LOHFT-pawst-free-mehr-ker?

419. Will it go out today?
Bliver det afsendt idag?
bleer dé OW-sent ee-DÄ?

420. I want to send a money order.
Jeg vil gerne sende en postanvisning.
yĭ vé gehr-neh sen-neh en PAWST-ÄN-vees-ning.

TELEGRAM AND CABLEGRAM
TELEGRAM OG KABELGRAM

421. Will you send [a cablegram]?
Vil De sende [et kabelgram]?
vé dee sen-neh [et KÄ-bel-gräm]?

422. —— a telegram.
et telegram.
et té-lé-GRÄM.

423. What is the word-rate to New York City?
Hvad er taksten pr. ord til New York City?
vä ehr TÄX-ten pehr OHR/ té New York City?

424. I will send this with "prepaid reply."
Jeg sender det med "svar betalt."
yĭ sen-ner dé meh SVAHR bé-tält.

425. When will it arrive?
Hvornår vil det ankomme?
vor-NAWR vé dé ÄN-kom-meh?

HOTEL
HOTEL

426. I am looking for [a good hotel].
Jeg søger [et godt hotel].
yĭ SÖR-wer [et GOT ho-TEL].

427. —— the best hotel.
det bedste hotel.
dé BEH-steh ho-TEL.

428. —— an inexpensive hotel.
et billigt hotel.
et BEEL-leet ho-TEL.

429. —— a boarding house.
et pensionat.
et pahng-sho-NÄ/t.

430. I (do not) want to be in the center of town.
Det skal (ikke) være i byens centrum.
dé skă (ig-eh) veh-reh ee bew-ens SEN-trŏŏm.

431. A place, where it is not noisy.
Et sted, hvor der ikke er støj.
et steth vor dehr ig-eh ehr STOY.

432. I have a reservation for today.
Jeg har bestilt værelse til idag.
yĭ hahr bé-STILT VEHR-el-seh té ee-DÄ.

433. Do you have [a room]?
Har De [et værelse]?
hahr dee [et VEHR-el-seh]?

434. —— a single room.
et enkeltværelse.
et ENKL/t-vehr-el-seh.

435. —— a double room.
et dobbeltværelse.
et DOPL/t-vehr-el-seh.

436. —— a suite.
en suite.
en SVEET-teh.

437. I want a room [with a double bed].
Jeg ønsker et værelse [med dobbeltseng].
yī ERN-sker et VEHR-el-seh [meh DOPL/t-seng].

438. —— with twin beds.
med to senge.
meh TOH seng-eh.

439. —— with a bath.
med bad.
meh BĂ/th.

440. —— with a shower.
med brusebad.
meh BROO-seh-bă/th.

441. —— with a sink.
med kumme.
meh KOHM-meh.

442. —— with hot water.
med varmt vand.
meh VAHRMT văn/.

443. —— **with a balcony.**
    med balkon.
    meh bäl-KONG.

444. I will take a room [for tonight].
    Jeg tager et værelse [for i nat].
    yĭ TAHR et VEHR-el-seh [for ee NĂT].

445. —— **for several days.**
    for flere dage.
    for FLÉ-reh DĂ-weh.

446. —— **for two persons.**
    til to personer.
    té TOH pehr-SOH-ner.

447. May I have it [with] without meals?
    Kan jeg faa det [med] uden pension?
    kă yĭ faw dé [METH] OO-then pahng-SHOHN?

448. What is the price per day?
    Hvad er prisen pr. dag?
    vă ehr PREE-sen pehr DĂ?

449. Are tax and service included?
    Er skat og betjening inkluderet?
    ehr SKĂT aw bét-YEH-ning in-klŏŏ-DÉ-reth?

450. I would like to see the room.
    Jeg vil gerne se værelset.
    yĭ vé gehr-neh SÉ VEHR-el-set.

451. I (do not) like this one.
    Jeg synes (ikke) om dette her.
    yĭ sewns (ig-eh) om det-teh hehr.

452. Have you something [better]?
    Har De noget [bedre]?
    hahr dee no-eth [BETH-reh]?

453. —— cheaper.
billigere.
BEEL-lee-eh-reh.

454. —— larger.
større.
STERR-reh.

455. —— smaller.
mindre.
MÉN-dreh.

456. A room facing [the street] the courtyard.
Et værelse [til gaden] til gården.
et VEHR-el-seh [té GÄ-then] té GAW-ren.

457. Lower down.   **458. Higher up.**
Længere nede.   Højere oppe.
LENG-er-eh NÉ-the.   *HOY-er-eh OP-eh.*

459. With more [light] air.
Med mere [lys] luft.
Meh mé-reh [lews/] lohft.

460. Upstairs.   Downstairs.
Ovenpå.   Nedenunder.
OW-en-paw.   Né-then-ohn-ner.

461. Is there an elevator?
Er der elevator?
ehr dehr é-lé-VÄ-tor?

462. What is my room number?
Hvad nummer er mit værelse?
vä NOHM/r ehr meet VEHR-el-seh?

463. Please sign the hotel register.
Vær så venlig at skrive Dem ind i hotellets bog.
*vehr saw ven-lee aw skree-veh dem IN/ ee ho-TEL-lets
baw.*

464. Please fill out this form.
Vær så venlig at udfylde denne blanket.
vehr saw ven-lee aw OOTH-fewl-leh den-neh blăng-KET.

465. May I have the key to my room?
Må jeg bede om nøglen til mit værelse?
maw yĭ bé om NOY-len té meet VEHR-el-seh?

466. Will you send [the chambermaid] up here?
Vil De sende [stuepigen] herop?
ve dee sen-neh [STOO-pee-en] hehr-OP?

467. —— **a bellhop.**
en piccolo.
en peek-o-lo.

468. —— **a porter.**
hotelkarlen.
ho-TEL-kă-len.

469. —— **a messenger.**
et bud.
et bŏŏth/.

470. Who is it?
Hvem er det?
vem ehr dé?

471. Will you [call me] wake me at 9 o'clock?
Vil De [kalde på mig] vække mig Klokken 9?
vé dee [kal-leh paw mĭ] vek-keh mĭ klok-ken NEE?

472. I would like to have breakfast in my room.
Jeg vil gerne have min morgenmad på værelset.
yĭ vé gehr-neh ha meen MORN-math paw VEHR-el-set.

473. I want to speak to the manager.
Jeg ønsker at tale med direktøren.
yĭ ERN-sker aw tă-leh meh dee-rek-TĒR-ren.

474. I wish to engage [a nurse] a babysitter.

Jeg ønsker at engagere [en barnepige] en "baby-sitter."

yĭ ERN-sker aw äng-gä-SHÉ-reh [en BAHR-neh-pee-eh] en "baby-sitter."

475. I am ill.

Jeg er syg.

yĭ ehr SEW.

476. I need a nurse.

Jeg må have en sygeplejerske.

Yĭ maw hä en SEW-eh-plĭ-er-skeh.

477. Are there any letters or messages for me?

Er der nogen breve eller besked til mig?

ehr dehr nohn BRÉ-veh el/r bé-SKÉTH té mĭ?

478. I am expecting [a visitor].

Jeg venter [besøg].

yĭ vent/r [bé-SERH].

479. —— a telephone call.

en telefonopringning.

en télé-FOHN-op-ring-ning.

480. —— a package.

en pakke.

en PAHK-keh.

481. When must the room be vacated?

Hvornår skal man være ude af værelset?

vor-NAWR skä män veh-reh OO-the ä VEHR-el-seth?

482. Make out my bill now as I am leaving immediately.

Skriv min regning ud nu, da jeg straks skal afsted.

skreev meen RĬ-ning ooth NÖÖ, dä yĭ STRAHKS skä ä-steth.

483. Will you accept my personal check?
Vil De akceptere min personlige check?
vé dee ăk-sep-TÉ-reh meen pehr-SOHN-lee-eh shek?

484. Will you forward my mail to American Express in Paris?
Vil De eftersende min post til American Express i Paris?
vé dee EFT/r-sen-neh meen pawst té "American Express" ee pah-REES?

CHAMBERMAID
STUEPIGE

485. I don't want to be disturbed until 7 o'clock.
Jeg vil ikke forstyrres før Klokken 7.
yĭ vé ig-eh for-STEWR-res fĕrr klok/n sewv.

486. [The door] the lock does not work well.
[Døren] låsen fungerer ikke ordentligt.
[DĔR-ren] LAW/-sen fohn-GÉ-rer ig-eh OR-den-leet.

487. The room is too [cold] hot.
Værelset er for [koldt] varmt.
VEHR-el-seth ehr for [KAWL/t] vahrm/t.

488. Could I have some things washed?
Kunde jeg få noget tøj vasket?
kŏŏ yĭ faw no-eth TOY vă-sketh?

489. Will you bring me another [blanket]?
Vil De bringe mig [et tæppe] til?
vé dee bring-eh mĭ [et TEP-peh] TÉL/?

490. —— a bath mat.
en bademåtte.
en BĂ-the-mawt-teh.

491. —— **some coat hangers.**
nogle bøjler.
nohn BOY-ler.

492. —— **a glass.**
et glas.
et gläs/.

493. —— **a pillow.**
en hovedpude.
en HOH-eth-poo-the.

494. —— **a cake of soap.**
et stykke sæbe.
et stĕrk-keh SEH-beh.

495. —— **some toilet tissue.**
noget toiletpapir.
no-eth toh-ă-LET-pă-peer/.

496. —— **some towels.**
nogle håndklæder.
nohn HON-klehr.

497. —— **some washcloths.**
nogle vaskeklude.
nohn VĂ-skeh-kloo-the.

498. —— **some drinking water.**
noget drikkevand.
no-eth DRIK-keh-vän/.

499. Will you change the sheets?
Vil De skifte lagnerne?
vé dee SKEEF-teh LAH-nehr-neh?

500. Will you make up my bed?
Vil De rede min seng?
vé dee RÉ meen seng/?

501. Will you come back later?
Vil De komme igen senere?
vé dee kom-meh ee-GEN sé-né-reh?

APARTMENT
LEJLIGHED

502. I am looking for a furnished apartment [with a bathroom].
Jeg søger en møbleret lejlighed [med badeværelse].
yī SĒR-wer en mēr-BLÉ-reth LĪ-lee-héth [meh BĂ-the-vehr-el-seh].

503. —— with two bedrooms.
med to soveværelser.
meh TOH| SOW-eh-vehr-el-şer.

504. —— with a dining room.
med en spisestue.
meh en SPEES-eh-stoo-eh.

505. —— with a kitchen.
med køkken.
meh KĒRK-ken.

506. —— with a living room.
med opholdsstue.
meh OP-hols-stoo-eh.

507. Do you furnish the [table linen] sheets, towels?
Leverer De også [dækketøj] lagner, håndklæder?
lé-VEH-rer dee os-seh [DEK-eh-toy] LAH-ner, HON-klehr?

508. —— the dishes.
porcelæn.
por-seh-LEN.

509. —— **the silverware.**
sølvtøj.
SERL-toy.

510. —— **the cooking utensils.**
kogeredskaber.
KAW-weh-réth-skäb/r.

511. Do you know a good [cook] housemaid?
Kender De en god [kokkepige] stuepige?
KEN/r dee en GO/ [kok-keh-pee-eh] STOO-pee-eh?

CAFÉ
PÅ KAFÉ

512. Bartender, I'd like to have [a drink].
Bartender, jeg vil gerne have [en drink].
bar-tender, yǐ vé gehr-neh hǎ [en drink].

513. —— **en "akvavit" (a schnaps) (Danish spirits flavored with caraway seeds).**
en akvavit (en snaps).
en ǎ-kvǎ-VEET (en snäps).

514. —— **a brandy.**
en cognak.
en KON-yäk.

515. —— **a cocktail.**
en cocktail.
en "cocktail."

516. —— **a fruit drink.**
en drik med frugtsaft.
en drik meh FROHKT-säft.

517. —— **a [small] large bottle of mineral water.**
en [lille] stor flaske mineralvand.
en [leel-leh] stohr flås-keh mee-neh-RAHL-văn/.

518. —— **some [light] dark beer.**
noget [lyst] mørkt øl.
no-eth [lewst] mĕrrkt ERL.

519. —— **champagne.**
champagne.
shäm-PĂN-yeh.

520. —— **a liqueur (cordial).**
en likør.
en lee-KERR.

521. —— **a glass of [port] sherry.**
et glas [portvin] sherry.
et glås [pohrt-veen] ''sherry.''

522. —— **a whiskey (and soda).**
en whisky (og soda).
en VEE-skee (aw SOH-dă).

523, —— **a bottle of [white wine] red wine.**
en flaske [Hvidvin] Rødvin.
en flås-keh [VEETH-veen] RERTH-veen.

524. Let's have another.
Lad os få een til.
lă os faw én/ tél/.

525. To your health!
Skål!
SKAWL/!

RESTAURANT
RESTAURANT

526. Can you recommend a good restaurant [for lunch]?

Kan De anbefale en god restaurant [for frokost]?

kä dee ÄN-bé-fä-leh en GO/ ré-sto-RAHNG [for FRO-kost]?

527. —— for supper.

for aftensmad.

for AHF-tens-mäth.

528. —— for a sandwich.

for et stykke smørrebrød.

for et stērk-keh SMĒRR-reh-brērth.

529. At what time is dinner served?

Hvad tid serveres middagen?

vä teeth sehr-VÉ-res mé-dä-n?

530. Can we [lunch] dine now?

Kan vi [spise frokost] spise middag nu?

kä vee [spee-seh FRO-kost] spee-seh mé-dä nöö?

531. Are you [the waiter] at this table?

Er De [tjener] ved dette bord?

ehr dee [tyeh-ner] vé det-teh BOHR?

532. —— the waitress at this table?

servitrice ved dette bord?

sehr-vee-TREE-seh vé det-teh BOHR?

533. Where is the headwaiter?

Hvor er overtjeneren?

vohr ehr OW/r-tyeh-neh-ren?

534. —— the wine steward.

kyperen.

KEWP-eh-ren.

535. Waiter!
Tjener!
TYEH-ner!

536. Give us a table [near the window].
Giv os et bord [ved vinduet].
gee os et BOHR [vé VIN-dŏŏ-eth].

537. —— outside.
udenfor.
OO-then-for.

538. —— inside.
indenfor.
IN-en-for.

539. —— at the side.
ved siden.
vé SEE-then.

540. —— in the corner.
i hjørnet.
ee YERR-neth.

541. —— for four persons.
til fire.
té FEE-reh.

542. Please serve us quickly.
Vær venlig og servere os hurtigt.
vehr ven-lee aw sehr-vé-reh os HŎŎR-teet.

543. We want to dine à la carte.
Vi vil gerne spise à la carte.
vee vél gehr-neh spee-seh à la carte.

544. We want to dine table d'hôte.
Vi tager den faste middag.
vee tahr den făs-teh mé-dă.

545. What is the specialty of the house?
Hvad er husets specialitet?
vă ehr HOO-sets spé-shă-lee-TÉT?

546. Will you bring me [the menu]?
Vil De bringe mig [spisekortet]?
vé dee bring-eh mĭ [SPEE-seh-kawr-teth]?

547. —— the wine list.
vinkortet.
VEEN-kawr-teth.

548. —— bread and butter.
brød og smør.
brĕrth aw smĕrr.

549. —— a fork.
en gaffel.
en GAHF/l.

550. —— a knife.
en kniv.
en k-neev.

551. —— a teaspoon.
en teske.
en TÉ-ské.

552. —— a large spoon.
en spiseske.
en SPEE-seh-ské..

553. —— a napkin.
en serviet.
en sehr-vee-YET.

554. —— a plate.
en tallerken.
en tă-LEHR-ken.

555. I prefer [ordinary, plain food].
Jeg foretrækker [almindelig, jævn mad].
yī FAW-reh-trek/r [ål-mén-neh-lee, yevn mäth].

556. —— food that is not too spicy.
mad, der ikke er for krydret.
math dehr ig-eh ehr for KRĒRTH-reth

557. —— food that is not too sweet.
mad, der ikke er for sød.
math dehr ig-eh ehr for SĒRTH.

558. —— food that is not too sour.
mad, der ikke er for sur.
math, dehr ig-eh ehr for SOOR.

559. —— food that is not too fat.
mad, der ikke er for fed.
math, dehr ig-eh ehr for FÉTH.

560. —— food that is not too tough.
mad, der ikke er for sejg.
math, dehr ig-eh ehr for SĪ/.

561. May I have a little [more] less?
Må jeg bede om lidt [mere] mindre
maw yī bé om lit [mé-ré] min-dreh?

562. I have eaten [enough] too much.
Jeg har spist [nok] for meget.
yī hahr speest [NOK] for MĪ-eth.

563. I prefer the meat [rare].
Jeg foretrækker kødet [rødt].
yī FAW-reh-trek/r KĒR-thet [rērth].

564. —— medium.
tilpas stegt.
té-PÄS stékt.

565. —— well done.
gennemstegt.
GEN-nem-stékt.

566. It is [overcooked] undercooked.
Det har [kogt for længe] ikke kogt længe nok.
dé hahr [kokt for LENG-eh] ig-eh kokt leng-eh NOK.

567. This is cold.
Dette her er koldt.
det-teh hehr ehr KOL/t.

568. Will you take it away?
Vil De tage det væk?
vé dee tä dé vek?

569. I did not order this.
Det dér har jeg ikke bestilt.
dé dehr hahr yĭ ig-eh bé-STILT.

570. May I have a salad instead?
Kan jeg få en salat i stedet for?
kä yĭ faw en sä-LÄT ee steh-thet for?

571. May I have the check?
Må jeg få regningen?
maw yĭ faw RĬ-ning-en?

572. Are the tip and service charge included? -
Er drikkepenge og alt andet inkluderet?
ehr drék-eh-peng-eh aw ält än-neth in-klöö-DÉ-ret?

573. I think there is a mistake in the bill.
Jeg tror der er en fejl på regningen.
yĭ trohr dehr ehr en FĬL/ paw RĬ-ning-en.

574. What are these charges for?
Hvad er disse poster for?
vä ehr dees-seh POS-ter for?

575. The food and service were excellent.
Maden og betjeningen var fortrinlige.
MĂ-then aw bé-TYEH-ning-en vahr for-TREEN-lee-eh.

576. Keep the change.
Behold resten.
bé-HOL| res-ten.

577. Hearty appetite!
God appetit!
GO| ăp-peh-TEET|!

FOOD LIST
FØDEVARER, MAD OG DRIKKE

578. Drinking water. Drikkevand. *drik-keh-văn.*

579. Water with ice. Isvand. *EES-văn.*

580. Water without ice. Vand uden is i. *văn OO-then ees ee.*

581. The bread. Brødet. *BRĒR-thet.*

582. The butter. Smørret. *SMĒRR-reth.*

583. The sugar. Sukkeret. *SOHK-reth.*

584. The salt. Saltet. *SĂL-teth.*

585. The pepper. Peberet. *PÉV-reth.*

586. The sauce. Sovsen. *SOW-sen.*

587. The oil. Olien. *OHL-yen.*

588. The vinegar. Eddiken. *EH-thee-ken.*

589. The mustard. Sennepen. *SÉ-nep|n.*

590. The garlic. Hvidløget. *VEETH-loy-eth.*

591. The ketchup. Ketchupen. *KETCH-ĕrp|n.*

BREAKFAST FOODS
MORGENMAD

592. May I have [a glass of fruit juice]?
Må jeg få [et glas frugtsaft]?
maw yĭ faw [et gläs FROHKT-säft]?

593. —— a glass of orange juice.
et glas appelsinsaft.
et gläs äpl-SEEN-säft.

594. —— a glass of tomato juice.
et glas tomatsaft.
et gläs toh-MÄT-säft.

595. —— some stewed prunes.
nogle kogte svedsker.
nohn KOK-teh své-sker.

596. —— some oatmeal porridge.
en portion havregrød.
en por-SHOHN HÄV-reh-grĕrth.

597. —— some toast and jam (marmalade).
noget ristet brød og syltetøj (marmelade).
no-eth rés-teth brĕrth aw SEWL-teh-toy (mahr-meh-LÄ-the).

598. —— some rolls.
nogle rundstykker.
nohn ROHN/-stĕrk/r.

599. I will order [an omelet].
Jeg vil bestille [en omelet].
yĭ vé bé-stil/-leh [en oh-meh-LET].

600. —— some soft-boiled eggs.
nogle blødkogte æg.
nohn BLĔRTH-kok-teh EG/.

601. —— **some four-minute eggs.**
nogle fire-minutters æg.
nohn FEE-reh mee-nōōd-ders EG/.

602. —— **some hard-boiled eggs.**
nogle hårdkogte æg.
nohn HAWR-kok-teh EG/.

603. —— **some fried eggs.**
nogle spejlæg.
nohn SPĪ-leh-eg/.

604. —— **an order of scrambled eggs.**
en gang røræg.
en gahng RĒRR-eg/.

605. —— **two orders of bacon and eggs.**
to gange ristet bacon og æg.
toh gäng-eh ris-teth bacon aw eg/.

606. —— **an order of ham and eggs.**
en gang ristet skinke og æg.
en gahng ris-teth skéng-keh aw eg/.

SOUPS AND ENTRÉES
SUPPE OG FORSKELLIGE RETTER

607. I want [chicken soup].
Jeg vil gerne have [hønsekødsuppe].
yī vé gehr-neh hä [HĒRN-seh-kērth-sohb-beh].

608. —— **vegetable soup.**
suppe med grøntsager.
sohb-beh GRĒRN-sä-wer.

609. —— **consommé.**
klar suppe.
klahr sohb-beh.

610. —— **some beef.**
noget oksekød.
no-eth OX-eh-kẽrth.

611. —— **roast beef.**
oksesteg.
OX-eh-stī/.

612. —— **broiled (chicken).**
grillstegt (kylling).
gril-stékt (kewl-ling).

613. —— **fried chicken.**
stegt kylling.
stékt kewl-ling.

614. —— **roast duck.**
andesteg.
ÅN-neh-stī/.

615. —— **roast goose.**
gåsesteg.
GAW-seh-stī/.

616. —— **hamburgers.**
hakkebøf.
HĂK-keh-bẽrf.

617. —— **hors d'œuvres.**
hors d'œvres.
or-DĒRV-rer.

618. —— **lamb roast.**
lammesteg.
LĂM-meh-stī/.

619. —— **lamb chops.**
lammekoteletter.
LĂM-meh-koht-eh-let-ter.

620. —— lamb stew.
lammefrikassé.
LĂM-meh-frik-kă-sé.

621. —— liver.
lever.
LÉ-vehr.

622. —— lobster.
hummer.
HOHM/r.

623. —— oysters.
østers.
ĒRS-ters.

624. —— roast pork.
flæskesteg.
FLEHS-keh-stī/.

625. —— sardines.
sardiner.
sahr-DEE-ner.

626. —— sausage.
pølse.
PĒRL-seh.

627. —— shrimp.
rejer.
RĪ-er.

628. —— steak.
engelsk bøf.
EHNG-elsk bĕf.

629. —— steak (garnished with butter that is mixed with chopped parsley).
fransk bøf.
frăn/sk bĕf.

630. —— **veal.**
kalvekød.
KĂL-veh-kērth.

VEGETABLES AND SALAD
GRØNTSAGER OG SALAT

631. Will you serve me [asparagus].
Vil De bringe mig [asparges].
vé dee bring-eh mĭ [ă-SPAHRS].

632. —— **cabbage.**
kål.
KAWL/.

633. —— **carrots.**
gulerødder.   (karotter.)
GOOL-leh-rērth-ther.   *(kă-ROT/r.)*

634. —— **cauliflower.**
blomkål.
BLOM-kawl.

635. —— **celery and olives.**
bladselleri og oliven.
BLĂTH-sé-lé-ree aw oh-LEE-ven.

636. —— **cucumber salad.**
agurkesalat.
ă-GOOR-keh-să-LĂT/.

637. —— **lettuce.**
grøn salat.
grērn să-LĂT/.

638. —— **mushrooms.**
champignons.
SHĂM-peen-yong.

639. —— **onions.**
løg.
loy/.

640. —— **peas.**
ærter.
EHR-ter.

641. —— **a boiled potato.**
en kogt kartoffel.
en kokt kär-TOF/l.

642. —— **a baked potato.**
en bagt kartoffel.
en bäkt kär-TOF/l.

643. —— **fried potatoes.**
stegte kartofler.
sték-teh kär-TOF-ler.

644. —— **mashed potato.**
kartoffelmos.
kär-TOFL-mohs.

645. —— **rice.**
ris.
rees/.

646. —— **spinach.**
spinat.
spee-NÄT/.

647. —— **string beans.**
snittebønner.
sneet-teh-bērn-er.

648. —— **tomatoes.**
tomater.
toh-MÄT/r.

FRUIT
FRUGT

649. Will you bring me [an apple].
Vil De bringe mig [et æble].
vé dee bring-eh mĭ [et EH-bleh].

650. —— some cherries.
nogle kirsebær.
nohn KEER-seh-behr.

651. —— a grapefruit.
en grape-frugt.
en grep-frohkt.

652. —— some grapes.
nogle vindruer.
nohn VEEN-droor.

653. —— some lemon.
noget citron.
no-eth see-TROHN.

654. —— a slice of melon.
et stykke melon.
et stērk-keh mé-LOHN.

655. —— an orange.
en appelsin.
en ăpl-SEEN.

656. —— a peach.
en fersken.
en FEHR-sken.

657. —— a pear.
en pære.
en PEH-reh.

658. —— **a portion of raspberries.**
en portion hindbær.
en por-SHOHN HIN-behr.

659. —— **a portion of strawberries.**
en portion jordbær.
en por-SHOHN YOHR-behr.

BEVERAGES
DRIKKE

660. I will have [a cup of black coffee].
Jeg vil gerne have [en kop sort kaffe].
yǐ vé gehr-neh hǎ [en kop SOHRT kǎf-feh].

661. —— **coffee with cream.**
kaffe med fløde.
kǎf-feh meh FLĒR-the.

662. —— **a pot of tea.**
en kande te.
en kǎn-neh TÉ/.

663. —— **a cup of hot chocolate.**
en kop chokolade.
en kop shoh-ko-LǍ-the.

664. —— **a glass of milk.**
et glas mælk.
et glǎs MELK/.

665. —— **a bottle of lemonade.**
en flaske limonade.
en flǎs-keh lee-mo-NǍ-the.

666. —— **a bottle of carbonated water.**
en sodavand.
en SO-dǎ-vǎn.

DESSERTS
DESSERTER

667. May I have [some cake]?
Må jeg få [noget kage]?
maw yĭ faw [no-eth KĀ-weh]?

668. —— some cheese.
noget ost.
no-eth OHST/.

669. —— some cookies.
nogle småkager.
nohn SMOK-kä-wer.

670. —— some caramel custard, vanilla custard.
noget karamelbudding, vanillebudding.
no-eth kä-rä-MEL-bōō-thing, vă-NEEL-yeh-bōō-thing.

671. —— some French pastry.
nogle konditorkager.
nohn kohn-DEE-tor-kä-wer.

672. —— a fruit tart.
en frugttærte.
en FROHKT-tehr-teh.

673. —— chocolate ice cream, vanilla ice cream.
en chokoladeis, en vanilleis.
en shoh-ko-LĂ-the-EES, en vă-NEEL-yeh-EES.

674. —— a piece of layer cake.
et stykke lagkage.
et stĕ̄r-keh LAH-kä-weh.

DANISH FOOD SUPPLEMENT: NATIVE FOODS AND CUSTOMS

The Danish cuisine is rich, varied and probably too starchy for most American tastes. Gradually more emphasis is being placed on raw vegetables and salads. Danes are great bread eaters and for breakfast and lunch you will find a wide assortment of breads and Danish pastries. Notice the names of the different breads as you will frequently be asked to write your choice of bread and any of the various fillings. The menu or list of open-faced sandwiches is called "en smørrebrødsseddel"; the wide variety of fillings "pålæg" (lit. onlay). Cold cuts, pastes, salads and cheeses are usually listed in a column on the left side of the sandwich list while vertical lines divide the right side, forming a box for each type of bread available.

In large restaurants a buffet table corresponding to "smörgåsbord" is commonly referred to as "Det store kolde bord" (the big cold table). This is presented for lunch, dinner or supper and usually followed by a hot entrée. Food from the cold table is invariably eaten in the following order: herring and other fish or shell delicacies, cold cuts, salads and cheeses. You change your plate after the fish and avoid heaping all foods together.

Danes have a favorite refreshment break called "Eftermiddagskaffe" (afternoon coffee). Almost a meal in itself, it is accompanied by cakes, cookies and pastries. Five o'clock tea can also be indulged in by those who prefer tea to coffee. Afternoon shoppers can have smaller meals and snacks in department store restaurants.

BREADS*

FORSKELLIGE SLAGS BRØD

675. En bolle.
en BAWL-leh.
A soft roll.

676. Franksbrød (lit. French bread).
fränsk-brĕrth.
A white bread with crunchy crust.

677. En kiks.
en kéks.
A cracker or biscuit.

678. Rugbrød; lyst, mørkt.
rōō-brĕrth; lewst, mĕrkt.
Pumpernickel; light, dark.

679. Et rundstykke.
et rohn-stĕrk-keh.
A hard roll.

680. Surbrød; Sigtebrød.
soor-brĕrth; sék-teh-brĕrth.
Ryebread.

681. Wienerbrød (lit. Vienna bread).
vee-nehr-brĕrth.
Danish pastry.

* All food lists have been alphabetized in Danish to facilitate the tourist's reading of Danish menus.

SANDWICH MENU*

SMØRREBRØDSSEDDEL OG PÅLÆG

2. Bøf tartar.
bĕrf tahr-TAHR.
Raw scraped beef mixed with raw egg yolk and capers.

Many of these dishes are accompanied by a fried egg, sliced hardboiled egg or cold, scrambled eggs.

683. Hakkebøf med løg.
häk-keh-berf meh loy.
Hamburger smothered in onions (cold).

684. Leverpostej.
lé-vehr-paw-stĭ.
Liverpaste.

685. Sprængt oksebryst.
sprengt ox-eh-brĕrst.
Slightly salted, boiled breast of beef.

686. Pølser.
pĕrl-ser.
Sausage (many varieties).

687. Rejemad.
rī-eh-mahth.
Tiny shrimp heaped on buttered pumpernickel (considered a special delicacy).

688. Rødbeder.
rĕrth-bé-thér.
Pickled sliced red beets.

689. Røget ål.
roy-eth awl.
Smoked eel.

690. Røget laks.
roy-eth lax.
Smoked salmon.

691. Rullepølse.
rŏŏl-leh-pĕrl-seh.
A specialty of spiced, pressed lamb.

692. Saltkød.
sahlt-kĕrth.
Corned beef.

693. Sild.
seel/.
Herring (served in a great number of ways with onions, eggs, pickled, marinated, smoked etc.).

694. Sildesalat.
seel-leh-sä-lät.
Herring salad (made of herring, beets, apples, onions, potatoes and all mashed to a smooth paste).

695. Skinke med røraeg.
skeng-keh meh rērr-eg.
Ham with scrambled eggs (cold).

696. Spegepølse.
spī-eh-pērl-seh.
Salami.

697. En [mild], skarp ost.*
en [meel], skahrp ohst.
A [mild] sharp cheese.

698. Fuldfed ost.
fōōl-féth-ohst.
A fat cheese.

699. En kabaret.
en kä-bä-RET.
A luncheon or supper consisting of "snitter" and a small hot dish, such as those described below.**

700. Snitter.
sneet/r.
Tea sandwiches (half-size open-faced sandwiches usually served at luncheon).

701. Tarteletter med hummer og asparges.
tahr-teh-LET/r meh hohm/r aw ä-spahrs.
Patty shells filled with a mixture of lobster and asparagus.

702. Krustader med skinke og grønærter.
kroo-stah-ther meh skéng-keh aw grērn-ehr-ter.
Croûtes with ham and green peas.

* At the bottom of the Smørrebrødsseddel the cheeses are listed. They are too numerous to describe here.

** This represents a typical luncheon served in a department store restaurant.

SOUPS*
SUPPER

703. Blåbærsuppe.
blaiw-behr-sohb-beh.
Blueberry soup.

* In addition to the usual soups, the daily Danish menu offers hot and cold fruit and bread soups.

704. Brødsuppe.
breth-sohb-beh.
Bread soup (made of white or dark bread with fruit juice and
raisins and garnished with whipped cream).

705. Hyldebærsuppe.
hewl-leh-behr-sohb-beh.
Elderberry soup.

706. Kærnemælkskoldskål.
KEHR-neh-melks-kol-skawl.
Cold buttermilk soup (made with beaten egg yolks and minced
lemon rind).

707. Kærnemælkssuppe.
kehr-neh-melks-sohb-beh.
Buttermilk soup (made with raisins, chopped almonds and
whipped cream).

708. Kørvelsuppe.
kerr-vel-sohb-beh.
Chervil soup (served with a poached egg).

709. Rabarbersuppe.
rä-bahr-behr-sohb-beh.
Rhubarb soup.

710. Hvid sagosuppe.
veeth sä-go-sohb-beh.
Sago-gruel soup (made with beaten egg yolks and sherry).

711. Sødsuppe.
serth-sohb-beh.
A sweet gruel soup (made on a base of barley, sago or tapioca
full of raisins, prunes, plums and sometimes dried apples and
pears—considered a Danish specialty).

712. Tykmælk.
tewk-melk.
Bonnyclabber (cold, curdled milk served with grated pumpernickel and brown sugar).

713. Æblesuppe.
eh-bleh-sohb-beh.
Apple soup.

714. Ærter gule.
ehr-ter goo-leh.
Yellow split pea soup (served with a dish of boiled side pork).

715. Øllebrød.
    ērl-leh-brērth.
    Beer and bread soup (pumpernickel diluted in beer and water
      boiled smooth and served with whipped cream).

DINNER DISHES
MIDDAGSRETTER

The Danish dishes listed below are served in good
boarding houses and provincial hotels. Luxury
hotels offer an international as well as a superb Danish
cuisine.

Vegetables and salads are neither as varied nor as
plentiful as they are in America, but they are fresh and
flavorful. As for the meat dishes, in addition to the
usual roasts of beef, lamb, veal, pork, chicken etc.,
there are many dishes of the meat loaf, stew and hash
variety that are very tasty. Creamy brown gravy and
candied or boiled potatoes are served with almost
every meat dish. Like the French, Danish cooks use
the organs such as hearts, brains, sweetbreads, kidneys
and liver.

HOT ENTRÉES
VARME RETTER

716. Bankekød.
    bäng-keh-kērth.
    Similar to Swiss steak.

717. Benløse fugle.
    bén-lēr-seh foo-leh.
    Boneless birds (a meat loaf imitation of game).

718. Biksemad med brunede kartofler.
bék-seh-mäth meh broo-neh-the kär-tof-ler.
Diced left over meat mixed with onions and served with
candied potatoes.

719. Blodpølse.
blohth-pĕrl-seh.
Fried blood sausage (pork) served with melted butter, cinna-
mon and sugar.

720. Brisler.
brees-ler.
Sweetbreads of veal.

721. Dyresteg.
dew-reh-stĭ.
Roast venison.

722. Fasaner.
fä-sä-ner.
Roast pheasant.

723. Forloren hare.
for-LOH-ren hah-reh.
Mock roast hare (made of meat loaf, larded and spiced).

724. Forloren skilpadde.
for-LOH-ren skél-pä-the.
Mock-turtle stew (made of calf's head, tongue, veal, small meat
balls and fish balls in a brown sauce).

725. Frikadeller.
fré-keh-del/r.
Large oval meat balls.

726. Fyldt hvidkålshoved.
fewlt veeth-kawls-hoh-eth.
Boiled cabbage stuffed with ground meat.

727. Gulasch.
goo-läsh.
Similar to Hungarian goulash.

728. Hachis.
hä-shee.
Hash with fried egg and candied potatoes.

729. Hakkebøf med løg.
häk-keh-bĕrf meh loy.
Hamburger smothered in onions.

730. Haresteg.
hah-reh-stĭ.
Roast hare.

731. Hjerter (stegte).
yehr-ter (stĕk-teh).
Hearts (roasted).

732. Høns i karry (eller peberrod).
hĕrns ee kahr-ree (el/r pé-ver-rohth).
Stewed chicken in curry or creamed horse-radish sauce.

733. Kalvekarbonade.
kahl-veh-kahr-boh-nă-the.
Vealburger.

734. Kåldolmer.
kawl-dol-mer.
Stuffed cabbage (made of ground pork and veal rolled in cabbage, boiled and sometimes fried).

735. Kyllinger (stegte).
kewl-ling-er (stĕk-teh).
Roast young chicken (generally stuffed with parsley).

736. Lammefrikassé.
lahm-meh-free-kă-sé.
Lamb stew with fresh vegetables.

737. Lobescoves.
lăbs-cows.
Stew (made of large pieces of beef prepared like goulash).

738. Lobescoves (skipper).
lăbs-cows.
Hash (made of slightly salted boiled beef with diced potatoes and onions in a brown sauce—a specialty in port restaurants).

739. Medisterpølse.
me-dee-ster-pĕr l-seh.
Pork sausage.

740. Ragout.
ră-g ŏŏ.
Stew.

741. Ruskomsnusk.
rohs-kom-sn ŏŏsk.
Hash (made of ham, carrots, potatoes, browned onions, bits of other meat and stirred in butter in a frying pan).

742. Ryper.
rew-per.
Roast grouse.

743. Svinemørbrad.
svee-neh-mērr-brā.
Pork tenderloin (fried or braised, stuffed with parsley or with apples and prunes).

FISH
FISK

744. Ål.
awl.
Eel (served boiled, fried, smoked, curried and in aspic—a real Danish specialty).

745. Fiskebudding med hummersovs.
fés-keh-booth-ing meh hohm-er-sows.
Fish pudding with lobster sauce (considered a special delicacy).

746. Flynder.
flēr-nehr.
Flounder.

747. Kogt gedde.
kawkt géth-the.
Boiled pike (usually served with a horse-radish and whipped cream sauce).

748. Kogt helleflynder.
kawkt hel-leh-flēr-nehr.
Boiled halibut (usually served with hollandaise sauce).

749. Laks.
lahks.
Salmon.

750. Laksørred.
lahks-ērr-reth.
Salmon trout.

751. Rødspætte (Frederikshavner).
Rēr-spet-teh.
Plaice (large and succulent—most famous from Frederikshavn).

752. Søtunge.
sēr-tohng-eh.
Sole.

753. Kogt torsk.
kawkt tawrsk.
Boiled cod (served with mustard sauce and melted butter).

754. Østers.
ĒR-sters.
Oysters.

DESSERTS
DESSERTER

Danish desserts are extensive. Custards, puddings, ice creams and mixtures of fruit and whipped cream abound. The number of French pastries is legion. Napoleons, Otellos (chocolate with custard inside), marzipan and cakes with whipped cream are extremely popular. Denmark is justly famed for her pastryshops (konditorier). Related to fruit soups but eaten as a dessert or refreshment are Danish fruit puddings (frugtgrød or rødgrød), served with milk or cream. Some have the consistency of jello or junket; others are more like a thick apple sauce.

755. Bondepige med slør.
bohn-neh-pee-eh meh slēr.
Peasant girl in a veil (made of pumpernickel crumbs browned in butter, mixed with grated chocolate, jam and topped with whipped cream).

756. Chokolade fromage med Flødeskum.
sho-ko-lãth-eh fro-mãsh meh flēr-the-skohm.
Chocolate pudding with whipped cream.

757. Konditorkager.
kohn-dee-tor-kah-wer.
French pastry.

758. Lagkage.
lah-kä-weh.
Layercake.

759. Linser.
lén-ser.
Tart (made of dough similar to shortbread and filled with almond paste).

760. Pandekager med syltetøj.
pän-neh-kä-wer meh sewl-teh-toy.
Pancakes and jam (tiny pancakes stuffed with strawberry jam and sprinkled with powdered sugar).

761. Rabarbergrød.
rah-bahr-behr-grērth.
Rhubarb pudding.

762. Ris a l'amande.
rees-ah-lä-mahng.
Rice pudding with whipped cream and almonds (served with a red, fruit sauce).

763. Rødgrød med fløde.
rērth-grērth meh-flēr-the.
Red pudding with cream (made of red currants and raspberries or some other combination of berries).

764. Sandkage.
sän-kä-weh.
Pound cake.

765. Smørkage.
smērr-kä-weh.
Rich Danish pastry.

766. Søsterkage.
sērs-ter-kä-weh.
Light raisin cake.

767. Stikkelsbærgrød.
sték-els-behr-grērth.
Gooseberry pudding.

768. Trifli.
treef-lee.
Trifle (made of sponge cake soaked in wine or liqueur, with macaroons, jam and whipped cream).

CHURCH
KIRKE

769. At what time is the [service] mass?
Hvad tid er der [gudstjeneste] messe?
vă teeth ehr dehr [GOOTHS-tyeh-neh-steh] MES-seh?

770. A Catholic church.
En katolsk kirke.
en kă-TOHL/sk keer-keh.

771. A Protestant church.
En protestantisk kirke.
en proh-teh-STĂN-teesk keer-keh.

772. A synagogue.
En synagoge.
en sew-nă-GOH-weh.

773. Is there an English-speaking [minister], rabbi, priest?
Er der en engelsk-talende [præst], rabbiner katolsk præst?
ehr dehr en EHNG-elsk-tă-len-eh [PREST], ră-BEE-ner, kă-TOHL/sk prest?

SIGHTSEEING
SE PÅ SEVÆRDIGHEDERNE

774. Where can I rent [a car]?
Hvor kan jeg leje [en bil]?
vohr kă yĭ LI-eh [en beel]?

775. —— a bicycle.
en cykel.
en seekl/.

776. —— **a horse and carriage.**
et hestekøretøj.
et HES-teh-kēr-reh-toy.

777. I want a licensed guide who speaks English.
Jeg ønsker en autoriseret turistfører, som taler engelsk.
yī ērn-sker en ow-toh-ree-SÉ-reth tōō-REEST/-fēr-rer, som tă-ler EHNG-elsk.

778. What is the charge [per hour] per day?
Hvad er taksten [pr. time] pr. dag?
vă ehr TĂX-den [pehr TEE-meh] pehr DĂ/?

779. What is the fare for a trip [to the island]?
Hvad koster en tur [over til øen]?
vă kos-ter en toor [ow/r té ĒR-en]?

780. —— **on the Jutland lakes (near the Himmel-**
bjerg).
på Himmelbjergssøerne.
paw HIML-byehrs-sēr-er-neh.

781. —— **to the sea.**
ud til havet.
ooth té HĂ-veth.

782. Call for me tomorrow at my hotel at 8 o'clock.
Hent mig på hotellet i morgen klokken 8 (otte).
HEN/t mī paw ho-TEL-leth ee MORN klok/n AW-teh.

783. Will you show me all the sights of interest?
Vil De vise mig alle seværdighederne?
vé dee vee-seh mī ăl-leh sé-VEHR-dee-hé-ther-neh?

784. I am interested in [architecture].
Jeg interesserer mig for [arkitektur].
yī in-tré-SÉ-rer mī for [AHR-kee-tek-toor].

785. —— **painting.**
malerkunst.
MĂ-ler-kohnst.

786. —— **sculpture.**
billedhuggerkunst.
BÉ-leth-ho-ger-kohnst.

787. —— **Danish arts and crafts.**
dansk kunsthåndværk.
dăn/sk KOHNST-hon-vehrk.

788. I would like to visit [the park].
Jeg vil gerne se [parken].
yĭ vé gehr-neh sé [PAHR-ken].

789. —— **the cathedral.**
domkirken.
DOM-keer-ken.

790. —— **the castle.**
slottet.
SLOT-eth.

791. —— **the library.**
biblioteket.
beeb-lee-oh-TÉ-keth.

792. —— **the monument.**
monumentet.
moh-nŏŏ-MEN-teth.

793. —— **the palace.**
paladset.
pă-LĂS-seth.

794. When does the museum [open] close?
Hvornår [åbner] lukker museet?
vor-NAWR [awb-ner] lohg/r mŏŏ-seh-eth?

795. Is this the way to [the entrance] the exit?
Er dette vejen til [indgangen] udgangen?
ehr det-teh VĪ-en té [IN-gahng-en] OOTH-gahng-en?

796. What is the price of admission?
Hvad koster entréen?
vă kos-ter ahng-TRÉ-en?

797. We would like to stop and see the view.
Vi vil gerne standse og se på udsigten.
vee vé gehr-neh STĂN-seh aw sé paw OOTH-sik-ten.

798. Will you take us back to the hotel?
Vil De bringe os tilbage til hotellet?
vé dee bring-eh os té-BĂ-weh té ho-TEL-leth?

799. If we have time, we shall visit the art gallery.
Hvis vi får tid, vil vi gå på kunstmuseet.
vés vee fawr teeth, vé vee gaw paw KOHNST-mŏŏ-seh-eth.

AMUSEMENTS
FORLYSTELSER

800. I would like to go to [a concert].
Jeg har lyst til at gå til [en koncert].
yĭ hahr lērst té aw gaw té [en kohn-SEHRT].

801. —— a ballet.
en ballet.
en bă-LET.

802. —— a gambling casino.
et spillekasino.
et SPIL-leh-kă-see-noh.

803. —— the folk dances.
en opvisning af folkedanse.
en OP-vees-ning ă FAWLK-eh-dăn-seh.

804. I would like to go to [the movies].
Jeg vil gerne i [biografen].
yĭ vé gehr-neh ee [bee-o-GRĂ-fen].

805. —— a night club.
på natklub.
paw NĂT-klōōb.

806. —— the opera.
i operaen.
ee OH-pé-rǎ-en.

807. —— the theater.
i teatret.
ee té-Ă-treth.

808. Where is the box-office?
Hvor er billetkontoret?
vohr ehr bee-LET-kohn-TOH-reth?

809. What is playing tonight?
Hvad går der iaften?
vǎ gawr dehr ee-AHFT/n?

810. Is there a matinee today?
Er der eftermiddagsforestilling idag?
ehr dehr EFT/r-mé-dǎs-FAW-reh-stil/-ing ee-DĂ/?

811. Have you any seats for tonight's performance?
Har De nogen billetter til aftenforestillingen?
hahr dee nohn bee-LET-ter té AHFT/n-FAW-reh-stil/-ing-en?

812. How much is [an orchestra seat]?
Hvad koster [en orkesterplads]?
vǎ kos-ter [en or-KES-ter-plăs]?

813. —— a balcony seat.
en plads på balkonen.
en plăs paw băl-KONG/n.

814. —— **a box.**
en loge.
en LOH-sheh.

**815. I prefer not to be [too near] too far away
from the stage.**
Jeg vil helst ikke være [for nær ved] for langt fra
scenen.
*yĭ vé helst ig-eh veh-reh [for NAIR/ vé] for LAHNKT
frå sé-nen.*

816. Will I be able to [see] hear well?
Vil jeg kunne [se] høre godt?
vé yĭ kŏŏn-neh [SÉ] HĒR-reh got?

817. May I have a program?
Må jeg få et program?
maw yĭ faw et pro-GRAHM/?

818. Can I rent opera glasses?
Kan jeg leje en teaterkikkert?
kă yĭ LĬ-eh en té-Ă-ter-keek-kert?

**819. When does [the evening performance] the
floor show begin?**
Hvornår begynder [aftenforestillingen] den sær-
lige optræden?
*vor-NAWR bé-GĒRN-ner [AHFT/n-FAW-reh-stil/-
ing-en] den SAIR-lee-eh OP-treh-then?*

820. How long is the intermission?
Hvor lang pause er der?
vor LAHNG POW-seh ehr dehr?

821. It was an [interesting] funny show.
Det var en [interessant] morsom forestilling.
*dé văr en [in-treh-SĂNT] MOHR-som FAW-reh-
stil/ing.*

822. Is there a cover charge?
Koster kuverten ekstra?
kos-ter kŏŏ-VEHR-ten EX-trä?

823. Is there a minimum charge?
Er der en minimumspris?
ehr dehr en MEE-nee-MŎŎMS-prees?

824. Where can we go to dance?
Hvor kan vi gå hen og danse?
vohr kǎ vee gaw hen aw DÅN-seh?

825. May I have this dance?
Må jeg danse med Dem?
maw yǐ DAHN-seh meh dem?

826. Will you play [a fox trot].
Vil De spille [en fox trot].
vé dee spil-leh [en fox trot].

827. —— a mambo.
en mambo.
en MÅM-bo.

828. —— a rumba.
en rumba.
en ROHM-bah.

829. —— a samba.
en samba.
en SÅM-bah.

830. —— a tango.
en tango.
en TAHNG-go.

831. —— a waltz.
en vals.
en väls/.

832. The music is excellent.
Musikken er storartet.
mŏŏ-SEEK/n ehr STOHR-ahr-teth.

SPORTS
SPORT

833. Let's go [to the beach].
Lad os tage [til stranden].
lä os tä [té STRÄN-nen].

834. —— to the swimming pool.
hen i svømmehallen.
hen/ ee SVĒRM-meh-HÄL-len.

835. —— to a soccer game.
til en soccer kamp.
té en soccer kämp/.

836. —— to the horse races.
til hestevæddeløb.
té HES-teh-veh-the-lērb.

837. —— to a tennis match.
til en tenniskamp.
té en tennis-kämp/.

838. —— to a gymnastics show.
til en gymnastikopvisning.
té en gewm-nă-STEEK/-OP-vees-ning.

839. I'd like to play [golf] tennis.
Jeg har lyst til at spille [golf] tennis.
yī hahr lērst té aw spil-leh [golf] tennis.

840. I need [some golf clubs].
Jeg må have [nogle golfkøller].
yī maw hă [nohn golf-kērl-ler].

841. —— a tennis racket.
en ketsjer.
en KET-sher.

842. —— some fishing tackle.
nogle fiskegrejer.
nohn fisk-eh-grĭ-er.

843. Can we go [fishing]?
Kan vi tage ud og [fiske]?
kă vee tă ooth aw [fisk-eh]?

844. —— horseback riding.
ride.
REE-the.

845. —— swimming.
svømme.
SVERM-meh.

846. —— skating.
løbe på skøjter.
lēr-beh paw SKOY-ter.

847. —— skiing.
stå på ski.
staw paw SKEE|.

BANK AND MONEY
BANK OG PENGE

848. Where is the nearest bank?
Hvor er den nærmeste bank?
vohr ehr den nehr-meh-steh BANK?

849. At which window can I cash this?
Ved hvilket vindue kan jeg hæve denne?
vé vil-keth VIN-dōō kă yĭ HAY-veh den-neh?

850. Will you cash a check?
Vil De indløse en check?
vé dee IN-lēr-seh en sheck?

851. I have [traveler's checks].
Jeg har [rejsechecks].
yĭ hahr [RĬ-seh-shecks].

852. —— a bank draft.
en bankanvisning.
en BANK-ĂN-vees-ning.

853. —— a letter of credit.
et akkreditiv.
et ă-kré-dee-TEEV.

854. —— a credit card.
et rejsekreditkort.
et RĬ-seh-kré-DEET-kort.

855. What is the exchange rate on the dollar?
Hvad er kursen for dollars?
vä ehr KŎOR-sen for DOL-lärs?

856. May I have thirty dollars' worth of Danish crowns?
Må jeg få tredive dollars i danske kroner?
maw yĭ faw TRETH-veh DOL-lärs ee dän-skeh kroh-ner?

857. Please change this for [some large bills].
Vær så venlig at bytte denne [i store sedler].
vehr saw ven-lee aw bewt-teh den-neh [ee STOH-reh seth-ler].

858. —— some small bills.
i små sedler.
ee SMAW|seth-ler.

859. —— **some small change.**
i småpenge.
ee SMAW-peng-eh.

860. I want to send fifty dollars to the U.S.
Jeg vil gerne sende halvtreds dollars til U.S.A.
*yĭ vé gehr-neh sen-neh häl-TRÉS/DOL-lärs té OO.
S. Ä.*

SHOPPING
GØRE INDKØB

861. I want to go shopping.
Jeg vil gerne gøre nogle indkøb.
yĭ veh gehr-neh gēr-reh nohn IN-kērp.

862. Will you take me to the shopping center.
Vil De køre mig hen i forretningskvarteret.
vé dee kēr-reh mĭ hen ee for-RET-nings-kvahr-TÉ-reth.

863. May I speak to [a salesman] a salesgirl?
Må jeg tale med [en ekspedient] en ekspeditrice?
maw yĭ tä-leh meh [en ex-péd-YENT] en ex-pé-dee-TREE-seh?

864. Is there anybody here who speaks English?
Er der nogen her, der taler engelsk?
ehr dehr nohn hehr, dehr tä-ler EHNG-elsk?

865. I am just looking around.
Jeg ser mig bare om.
yĭ SÉR/ mĭ bahr om.

866. How much is it [for each piece]?
Hvad koster det [stykket]?
vä kos-ter dé stērk-keth?

867. —— per meter.
meteren.
MÉ-té-ren.

868. —— all together.
ialt.
ee-ÄLT.

869. It is too expensive.
Det er for dyrt.
dé ehr for dewrt.

870. Is that your lowest price?
Er det Deres laveste pris?
ehr dé deh-res lä-veh-steh prees?

871. Is there [a discount] a guarantee?
Er der [rabat] garanti?
ehr dehr [rä-BÄT] gä-rahn-TEE?

872. The price is satisfactory.
Prisen passer mig.
PREE-sen päs/r mī.

873. I [do not] like that.
Det synes jeg [ikke] om.
dé sewns yī [ig-eh] om.

874. I prefer something [better].
Jeg foretrækker noget [bedre].
yī FAW-reh-trek/r no-eth [beth-reh].

875. —— cheaper.
billigere.
BEE-leeh-reh.

876. —— at a moderate price.
til en mellempris.
té en MEL-lem-prees.

877. —— **finer.**
finere.
FEE-neh-reh.

878. —— **plainer.**
mere almindeligt.
mé-reh äl-MÉN-eh-leet.

879. —— **softer.**
blødere.
BLER-the-reh.

880. —— **stronger.**
stærkere.
STEHR-keh-reh.

881. —— **looser.**
løsere.
LER-seh-reh.

882. —— **tighter.**
mere snævert.
mé-reh SNEV-ert.

883. —— **of medium size.**
i en mellemstørrelse.
ee en MEL-lem-sterr-rel-seh.

884. **Show me some others in a different style.**
Vis mig nogle i en anden façon.
vees mī nohn ee en ÄN-nen fä-SONG.

885. **May I try it on?**
Må jeg prøve den?
maw yī PRER-veh den?

886. **Will it [fade] shrink in washing?**
Vil den [falme] krybe i vask?
vé den [FÄL-meh] KREW-beh ee väsk?

887. It is [not] becoming to me.
Den klæder mig [ikke].
den KLAIR/ mĭ [ig-eh].

888. It does [not] fit.
Den passer [ikke] godt.
den PĂS-ser [ig-eh] GOT.

889. May I order one?
Kan jeg bestille én?
kă yĭ bé-STIL-leh én?

890. How long will the alterations take?
Hvor længe vil forandringerne tage?
vor-LENG-eh vé for-ĂN-dring-er-neh tă?

891. I shall come back later.
Jeg kommer igen senere.
yĭ kom-mer ee-GEN sé-neh-reh.

892. Will you wrap this?
Vil De pakke det ind?
vé dee păg-geh dé IN/?

893. I shall take it with me.
Jeg tager det selv med.
yĭ tar dé sel/ meh.

894. Do I pay at the cash register?
Betaler jeg ved kassen?
bé-TĂ-ler yĭ vé KĂS-sen?

895. Can you deliver it to my hotel?
Kan De sende det hen på mit hotel?
kă dee sen-neh dé hen paw meet ho-TEL?

896. It is fragile.
Det går let istykker.
dé gawr let ee-STE̅RK/r.

897. Handle with care!
Tag forsigtigt på det!
Tă for-SIK-tëet paw dé!

898. Pack it for export.
Pak det for eksport.
păk dé for ex-PORT.

899. Ship it by freight to Philadelphia.
Send det som fragtgods til Philadelphia.
sen/ dé som FRAHKT-gohs té Phila-DEL/-phia.

900. Will you give me [a bill]?
Vil De give mig [en regning]?
vé dee gee mĭ [en RĬ-ning]?

901. —— a receipt.
en kvittering.
en kvee-TÉ-ring.

902. —— a sales slip.
en nota.
en NOH-tă.

903. You will be paid on delivery.
De bliver betalt, når varerne er leveret.
dee bleer bé-tălt, nawr vah-rer-neh ehr lé-vé-reth.

904. Are there any other charges?
Er der andre poster at betale?
ehr dehr AHN-dreh pos-ter aw bé-tă-leh?

MEASUREMENTS
MÅL

905. Will you take my measurements?
Vil De tage mål af mig?
vé dee tă mawl/ ă mĭ?

906. What is [the size]?
Hvad er [størrelsen]?
vă ehr [STERR-rel-sen]?

907. —— the length.
længden.
LENG-den.

908. —— the width.
vidden (bredden).
VEE-den (BRÉ-den).

909. —— the weight.
vægten.
VEK-ten.

910. It is 7 meters long by 4 meters wide.
Den er 7 meter lang og 4 meter vid (bred).
den ehr sewv mé-ter lahng aw fee-reh meter vee/ (bréth).

911. Small. Lille. *LEEL-leh.*

912. Smaller. Mindre. *MÉN-dreh.*

913. Large. Stor. *stohr.*

914. Larger. Større. *stérr-reh.*

915. High. Høj. *hoy/.*

916. Higher. Højere. *hoy-eh-reh.*

917. Low. Lav. *lăv/.*

918. Lower. Lavere. *lă-veh-reh.*

919. Long. Lang. *lahng.*

920. Longer. Længere. *leng-eh-reh.*

921. Short. Kort. *kort.*

922. Shorter. Kortere. *kor-teh-reh.*

923. Thin. Tynd. *tērn/.*

924. Thinner. Tyndere. *tēr-neh-reh.*

925. Thick. Tyk. *tewk.*

926. Thicker. Tykkere. *tewk-eh-reh.*

927. Narrow. Smal. *smăl/.*

928. Narrower. Smallere. *smăl-leh-reh.*

929. Wide. Vid (bred). *vee/ (bréth).*

930. Wider. Videre (bredere). *vee-eh-reh (bré-the-reh).*

931. Old. Gammel. *gäml.*

932. Older. Ældre. *el-dreh.*

933. New. Ny. *new/.*

934. Newer. Nyere. *new/eh-reh.*

COLORS
FARVER

935. I want [a lighter] a darker shade.
Jeg ønsker [en lysere] en mørkere schattering.
yĭ ērn-sker [en lew-seh-reh] en mērr-keh-reh shä-TÉ-ring.

936. Black. Sort. *sohrt.*

937. Blue. Blå. *blaw/.*

938. Brown. Brun. *broon/.*

939. Cream. Flødefarvet. *flēr-the-fahr-veth.*

940. Gray. Grå. *graw/.*

941. Green. Grøn. *grērn/.*

942. Orange. Orangefarvet. *oh-RAHNG-sheh-fahr-veth.*

943. Pink. Lyserød. *LEWS-seh-rērth.*

944. Purple. Purpurrød. *pŏŏr-pŏŏr-rērth.*
Violet. *vee-o-LET.*

945. Red. Rød. *rērth.*

946. White. Hvid. *veeth.*

947. Yellow. Gul. *gool/.*

STORES
FORRETNINGER: BUTIKKER

948. Can you direct me to [an antique shop]?
Kan De sige mig, hvor der er [en antikvitets-
forretning]?
*kä dee see-eh mĭ, VOHR dehr ehr [en ăn-tee-kvee-TÉTS-
for-ret-ning]?*

949. —— a bakery.
et bageri.
et bä-weh-REE.

950. —— a bookshop.
en boghandel.
en BAW-hăn/l.

951. —— a butcher.
en slagter.
en SLAHKT/r.

952. —— a candy store.
en chokoladeforretning.
en shoh-koh-LĂ-the-for-ret-ning.

953. —— a cigar store.
en cigarhandel.
en see-GAHR-hăn/l.

954. —— a clothing store.
et klædemagasin.
et kleh-the-mä-gä-SEEN.

955. —— a delicatessen.
en viktualieforretning.
en veek-too-A-lee-eh-for-ret-ning.

956. —— a department store.
et stormagasin.
et STOHR-ma-ga-SEEN.

957. —— **a dressmaker.**
en dameskræderinde.
en DÄ-meh-skreh-the-rin-neh.

958. —— **a drugstore.** *
et apotek.
et a-poh-TEK.

959. —— **an outlet (notions) store.**
et billigt varehus.
et bee-leet VAH-reh-hoos.

960. —— **a florist shop.**
en blomsterhandel.
en BLOM-ster-hän/l.

961. —— **a fruit and vegetable store.**
en frugt-og-grønthandel.
en frohkt-aw-grēērnt-hän/l.

962. —— **a grocery.**
en urtekramhandel.
en OOR-teh-krahm-han/l.

963. —— **a grocer's shop.**
en kolonialhandler.
en KO-lo-nee-ä-hänl/r.

964. —— **a haberdashery.**
en herreekviperingsforretning.
en HEHR-reh-é-kvee-PÉ-rings-for-ret-ning.

965. —— **a hardware store.**
en isenkramforretning.
en EES-sen-kräm-for-ret-ning.

---

* In Denmark a drugstore serves as a pharmacy filling prescriptions, selling drugs, remedies, toiletries, etc. Many of the miscellaneous products sold in American drugstores can be purchased at a Danish "Sæbehus" (lit. a soap house).

966. —— **a hat shop.**
en hatteforretning.
en HĂT-teh-for-ret-ning.

967. —— **a jewelry store.**
en juvelérforretning.
en yōō-vé-LÉR-for-ret-ning.

968. —— **a liquor store.**
en vinhandel.
en VEEN-hăn/l.

969. —— **a market.**
en torvehal.
en TOR-veh-hăl.

970. —— **a meat market.**
et kødtorv *or* kødudsalg.
et KĔRTH-torv or KĔRTH-ooth-săl.

971. —— **a vegetable market.***
et grønttorv.
et GRĔRNT-torv.

972. —— **a milliner.**
en modehandlerinde.
en MOH-the-hăn-leh-rin-neh.

973. —— **a music shop.**
en musikhandel.
en mōō-SEEK-hăn/l.

974. —— **a shoemaker.**
en skomager.
en SKO-mă-wer.

975. —— **a shoe store.**
en skotøjsforretning.
en SKO-toys-for-ret-ning.

* A colorful sight in Copenhagen.

976. —— **a tailor.**
    en skrædder.
    en skreth-ther.

977. —— **a toy shop.**
    en legetøjsbutik.
    en LĪ-eh-toys-bōō-teek.

978. —— **a watchmaker.**
    en urmager.
    en OOR-mä-wer.

CIGAR STORE
"CIGAR OG TOBAKSHANDEL"

979. Is the cigar store open?
    Er cigarhandlen åben?
    ehr see-GAHR-hän-len AW-ben?

980. I want to buy [some cigars].
    Jeg vil gerne købe [nogle cigarer].
    yĭ vé ger-neh kēr-beh [nohn see-GAH-rer].

981. —— **a pack of American cigarettes.**
    en pakke amerikanske cigaretter.
    en pahk-keh ä-mé-ree-KÄN/-skeh see-gah-RET/r.

982. —— **a cigarette case (leather).**
    et cigaretetui (af læder).
    et see-gah-RET-é-tvee (ä LEH-ther).

983. —— **a pipe.**
    en pibe.
    en PEE-beh.

984. —— **some pipe tobacco.**
    noget pibetobak.
    no-eth PEE-beh-toh-bahk/.

985. —— **a lighter.**
en tænder.
en ten-ner.

986. —— **some lighter fluid.**
noget tændervædske.
no-eth ten-ner-ves-keh.

987. —— **a flint.**
en sten.
en sté/n.

DRUGSTORE
APOTEK

988. Where is there a drugstore where they understand English?
Hvor er der et apotek, hvor man forstår engelsk?
vohr ehr dehr et ä-poh-TÉK, vohr män for-STAWR EHNG-elsk?

989. Can you fill this prescription immediately?
Kan De ekspedere denne recept med det samme?
kä dee ex-pé-DÉ-reh den-neh ré-SEPT meh dé sam-meh?

990. Do you have [some adhesive tape]?
Har De [noget hefteplaster]?
hahr dee [no-eth HEF-teh-pläs-ter]?

991. —— **some alcohol.**
noget hospitalssprit.
no-eth hoh-spee-TÄL-spreet.

992. —— **an antiseptic.**
et antiseptisk middel.
et ante-SEP-teesk mee-thel.

993. —— **some aspirin.**
noget aspirin.
no-eth ä-spee-REEN.

994. —— **some bandages.**
bandager.
băn-DÄ-sher.

995. —— **some bicarbonate of soda.**
noget tvekulsurt natron.
no-eth tvé-kohl-sŏŏrt NÄ-tron.

996. —— **some boric acid.**
noget borsyre.
no-eth BOHR-sew-reh.

997. Do you have [a jar of cold cream]?
Har De [en krukke koldcreme]?
hahr dee [en krohk-keh kol-krehm]?

998. —— **a comb.**
en kam.
en kä/m.

999. —— **some corn pads.**
nogle ligtorneplastre.
nohn LEE-tohr-neh-pläs-treh.

1000. —— **a deodorant.**
et lugtfjernende middel.
et LOHKT-fyehr-nen-eh mee-thel.

1001. —— **a depilatory.**
et hårfjernende middel.
et HAWR-fyehr-nen-eh mee-thel.

1002. —— **some ear stoppers.**
nogle ørepropper.
nohn ER-reh-prop/r.

1003. —— **an eyecup.**
et øjenglas.
et OYN-gläs.

1004. —— **a box of face tissues.**
en æske ansigtsservietter.
en EH-skeh ÄN-sikts-sehr-vee-yet/r.

1005. —— **some gauze.**
gazebind.
GÄ-seh-bin/.

1006. —— **some hand lotion.**
en håndlotion.
en HON-lo-SHOHN.

1007. —— **a hairbrush.**
en hårbørste.
en HAWR-bērr-steh.

1008. —— **some hairpins.**
nogle hårnåle.
nohn HAWR-naw-leh.

1009. —— **a hot-water bottle.**
en varmedunk.
en VAHR-meh-dohnk.

1010. —— **an icebag.**
en ispose.
en EES-poh-seh.

1011. —— **some insect repellent.**
noget insektpulver.
no-eth in-SECT-pohl-ver.

1012. —— **some iodine.**
noget jod.
no-eth yohth.

1013. —— **a laxative (mild).**
et afføringsmiddel (mildt).
et OW-fer-rings-mee-thel (mee/lt).

1014. —— **a lipstick.**
en læbestift.
en LEH-beh-stéft.

1015. —— **a medicine dropper.**
en dråbetæller.
en DRAW-beh-tel/r.

1016. —— **a mouthwash.**
noget til at skylle munden med.
no-eth té aw skēīl-leh MOHN/en meh.

1017. —— **a nail file.**
en neglefil.
en NI-leh-feel.

1018. —— **some nail polish.**
noget neglelak.
no-eth NI-leh-lahk/.

1019. —— **some nail polish remover.**
noget neglelak-fjerner.
no-eth NÍ-leh-lahk-FYEHR-ner.

1020. —— **some hydrogen peroxide.**
noget brintoverilte.
no-eth BRINT-ow-er-eel-teh.

1021. —— **some face powder.**
noget pudder.
no-eth POO/-ther.

1022. —— **some talcum powder.**
noget talkum.
no-eth tăl-kŏŏm.

1023. —— **a razor.**
en barbermaskine.
en bahr-BÉR-mä-skee-neh.

1024. —— **a package of razor blades.**
en pakke barberblade.
en pahk-keh bahr-BÉR-blä-the.

1025. —— **some rouge.**
noget sminke.
no-eth SMING-keh.

1026. —— **some safety pins.**
nogle sikkerhedsnåle.
nohn SIK/r-héths-naw-leh.

1027. —— **sanitary napkins.**
hygiejnebind.
hew-gee-I-neh-bin/.

1028. —— **a sedative.**
et beroligende middel.
et bé-ROH-lee-neh mee-thel.

1029. —— **a shampoo.**
en champoing.
en SHÄM-poh-eng.

1030. —— **some shaving cream (brushless).**
noget barbercreme (brushless).
no-eth bahr-BÉR-krem ("brushless").

1031. —— **some shaving lotion.**
noget barbersprit.
no-eth bahr-BÉR-spreet/.

1032. —— **smelling salts.**
lugtesalt.
LOHK-teh-sălt.

1033. —— **a bar of soap.**
et stykke vaskesæbe.
et stērk-keh VĂS-keh-seh-beh.

1034. —— **a cake of soap.**
et stykke håndsæbe.
et stērk-keh HON-seh-beh.

1035. —— **some soap flakes.**
nogle sæbespåner.
nohn SEH-beh-sponr.

1036. —— **a pair of sunglasses.**
et par solbriller.
et păr SOHL-brélr.

1037. —— **sunburn ointment.**
salve mod solbrændthed.
săl-veh mohth SOHL-brent-héth.

1038. —— **suntan oil.**
en sololie.
en SOHL-ohl-yeh.

1039. —— **a thermometer.**
et termometer.
et tehr-moh-MÉ-ter.

1040. —— **a toothbrush.**
en tandbørste.
en TĂN-bērr-steh.

1041. —— **a tube of toothpaste.**
en tube tandpasta.
en too-beh TĂN-păs-tă.

1042. —— **a can of toothpowder.**
en dåse tandpulver.
en DAW-seh TĂN-pohl-ver.

CLOTHING STORE
KLÆDEMAGASIN

1043. I want to buy [a bathing cap].
Jeg vil gerne købe [en badehætte].
yĭ vé gehr-neh kēr-beh [en BĂ-the-het-teh].

1044. —— a bathing suit.
en badedragt.
en BĂ-the-drahkt.

1045. —— a belt.
et bælte.
et bel-teh.

1046. —— a blouse.
en bluse.
en BLOO-seh.

1047. —— a brassiere.
en brystholder.
en BRĒRST-holr.

1048. —— a coat.
en frakke.
en FRAHG-geh.

1049. —— a collar (ladies').
en krave.
en KRAH-veh.

1050. —— a collar (man's).
en flip.
en flip.

1051. —— some diapers.
nogle bleer.
nohn blér.

1052. —— a dress.
en kjole.
en KYOH-leh.

1053. —— some children's dresses.
nogle barnekjoler.
nohn BAHR-neh-kyoh-ler.

1054. —— **a garter belt.**
en strømpeholder.
en STRERM-peh-hol-r.

1055. —— **a pair of garters.**
et par strømpebånd.
et pår STRERM-peh-bon .

1056. —— **a girdle.**
et lille korset.
et leel-leh kor-SET.

1057. —— **a handbag.**
en håndtaske.
en HON-tås-keh.

1058. —— **a few handkerchiefs.**
nogle få lommetørklæder.
nohn FAW LOM-meh-terr-klehr.

1059. —— **a hat.**
en hat.
en hat.

1060. —— **a fur jacket.**
en pelsjakke.
en PELS-yahk-keh.

1061. —— **some lingerie.**
noget lingeri.
no-eth léng-shé-REE.

1062. —— **some neckties.**
nogle slips.
nohn slips.

1063. —— **a nightgown.**
en natkjole.
en NĀT-kyoh-leh.

1064. —— **a pair of panties.**
et par damebenklæder.
et pår DĀ-meh-bén-klehr.

1065. —— **a pair of pajamas.**
en pyjamas.
en pew-YĀ-mås.

1066. —— **a petticoat.**
et underskørt.
et OHN/r-skērrt.

1067. —— **a raincoat.**
en regnfrakke.
en RĪN-frahg-geh.

1068. —— **a robe (man's).**
en slåbrok.
en SLOB-rok.

1069. —— **a robe (ladies').**
en housecoat.
en "housecoat".

1070. —— **a bath robe.**
en badekåbe.
en BÄ-the-kaw-beh.

1071. —— **a scarf.**
et halstørklæde.
et HÄLS-tērr-kleh-the.

1072. —— **a pair of shoes.**
et par sko.
et pär SKOH.

1073. —— **shoelaces.**
skobånd.
SKOH-bon/.

1074. —— **a pair of shorts.**
et par shorts.
et pär "shorts".

1075. —— **a skirt.**
en nederdel.
en NÉ-ther-dél.

1076. —— **a slip.**
en underkjole.
en OHN/r-kyoh-leh.

1077. —— **a pair of slippers.**
et par hjemmesko.
et pär YEM-meh-skoh.

1078. —— **six pairs of socks.**
seks par sokker.
sex pär SOK/r.

1079. —— **a pair of (nylon) stockings.**
et par (nylon) strømper.
et par (NĪ-lon) strēm-per.

1080. —— **a suit (for ladies).**
en spadseredragt.
en spä-SÉ-reh-drahkt.

1081. —— **a suit (man's).**
et sæt tøj.
et set TOY.

1082. —— **a pair of suspenders.**
et par seler.
et pår SÉ-ler.

1083. —— **a sweater.**
en sweater.
en SVET-er.

1084. —— **a pair of trousers.**
et par herrebenklæder.
et par HEHR-reh-bén-klehr.

BOOKSHOP AND STATIONER*
BOGHANDEL OG PAPIRHANDEL

1085. Where is there [a bookshop]?
Hvor er der [en boghandel]?
vohr ehr dehr [en BAW-hän/l]?

1086. —— **a stationer.**
en papirhandler.
en pä-PEER-hän-ler.

1087. —— **stationery.**
papir.
pä-PEER.

1088. —— **a newsdealer.**
en aviskiosk.
en ä-VEES-kee-osk.

1089. I want to buy [a book].
Jeg vil gerne købe [en bog].
yĭ vé gehr-neh kȇr-beh [en baw].

* In Denmark this is usually seen as BOG-og-PAPIRHANDEL.

1090. —— **a guidebook.**
en rejsefører (Bädecker).
en RĪ-seh-fẽr-rer (beh-deh-ker).

1091. —— **some blotting paper.**
noget klatpapir.
no-eth klät-pā-PEER.

1092. —— **an assortment of picture postcards.**
et udvalg af prospektkort.
et OOTH-väl ä pro-SPEKT-kort.

1093. —— **a deck of playing cards.**
et spil kort.
et spil KAWRT.

1094. —— **an English-Danish dictionary.**
en engelsk-dansk ordbog.
en ehng-elsk-dän/sk OHR-baw.

1095. —— **one dozen envelopes.**
et dusin konvolutter.
et dōō-SEEN kon-veh-LOOD/r.

1096. —— **an eraser.**
et viskelæder.
et VISK-eh-lehr.

1097. —— **some ink.**
noget blæk.
no-eth blek.

1098. —— **some magazines.**
nogle ugeblade (magasiner).
nohn OO-eh-blä-the (mä-gä-SEE-ner).

1099. —— **a map of Denmark.**
et Danmarkskort.
et DÄN-marks-kawrt.

1100. —— **some artist's materials.**
nogle tegne-og-malerekvisitter.
nohn TĪ-neh-aw-MÄ-leh-ré-kvee-seet/r.

1101. —— **a newspaper.**
en avis.
en ä-VEES.

1102. —— **some carbon paper.**
noget karbonpapir.
no-eth kar-BONG-pah-peer.

1103. —— **some tissue paper.**
noget silkepapir.
no-eth silk-eh-pā-peer.

1104. —— **a sheet of wrapping paper.**
et ark indpakningspapir.
et ahrk IN-pahk-nings-pā-peer.

1105. —— **some typewriting paper.**
noget maskinskrivningspapir.
no-eth mä-SKEEN-skreev-nings-pā-peer.

1106. —— **a typewriter ribbon.**
et farvebånd.
et FAHR-veh-bon/.

1107. —— **a fountain pen.**
en fyldepen.
en FEWL-leh-pen/.

1108. —— **a pencil.**
en blyant.
en BLEW-änt.

1109. —— **some string.**
noget sejlgarn.
no-eth SĪL-gahrn.

1110. —— **a roll of Scotch tape.**
en rulle klæbestrimler.
en rōōl-leh KLEH-beh-strim-ler.

PHOTOGRAPHY
FOTOGRAFERING

1111. I want a roll of movie film for this camera.
Jeg vil gerne have en rulle smalfilm til dette
fotografiapparat.
*yī vé gehr-neh hā en rōōl-leh smahl-feelm té det-teh
fo-toh-grä-FEE-äp-pä-RĀT.*

1112. Have you any [color film] flashbulbs?
Har De [farvefilm] magniumsbomber?
hahr dee [fahr-veh-feelm] MAH-nee-ohms-bohm-ber?

1113. The size is ——.

Størrelsen er ——.

STĒRR-rel-sen ehr ——.

1114. What is the charge [for developing a roll]?

Hvad er prisen [for at fremkalde en rulle]?

vä ehr pree-sen [for aw frem-käl-leh en rool-leh]?

1115. —— for one print of each.

pr. aftryk.

pehr OW-trĕrk.

1116. —— for an enlargement.

for en forstørrelse.

for en for-STĒRR-rel-seh.

1117. Will you have this ready for me as soon as possible.

Vil De have dette færdigt til mig så hurtigt som muligt.

vé dee hå det-teh fehr-deet té mī saw HŌO͞R-teet som moo-leet.

1118. May I take [a snapshot] some movies of you?

Må jeg tage [et knips] nogle levende billeder af Dem?

maw yī tå [et knips] nohn lé-ven-neh bil-ther ä dem?

BARBER SHOP AND BEAUTY PARLOR
BARBERSTUE OG FRISORSALON

1119. Where is there [a good barber] a hairdresser?

Hvor er der [en god barber] en frisør?

vohr ehr dehr [en GO/ bahr-BÉR] en free-sĕrr/?

1120. —— **a beauty parlor and ladies' hairdresser.**
en skønhedssalon og en damefrisør.
*en SKERN-héths-să-long aw en DĂ-meh-fr
serr.*

1121. I want [a haircut].
Jeg vil gerne have [håret klippet].
yĭ vé gehr-neh hă [HAW-reth klip-eth].

1122. —— **a facial.**
en ansigtsbehandling.
en ĂN-sikts-bé-HĂN-ling.

1123. —— **a massage.**
massage.
mă-SĂ-sheh.

1124. —— **a hair set.**
en vandondulering.
en VĂN-ong-dŏŏ-lé-ring.

1125. —— **a hair tint.**
håret tonet.
HAW-reth toh-neth.

1126. —— **a henna rinse.**
skyllet med henna.
skerl-leth meh HEN-nă.

1127. —— **a manicure.**
en manicure.
en mă-nee-KEW-reh.

1128. —— **a permanent wave.**
en permanent.
en pehr-mă-NENT.

1129. Can you do it now?
Kan De gøre det nu?
kă dee GER-reh dé NŎŎ?

1130. Can I make an appointment for tomorrow?
Kan jeg bestille tid til i morgen?
kä yĭ bé-stil-leh TEETH té ee morn?

1131. I part my hair [on this side].
Jeg har min skilning [i denne side].
yĭ hahr meen skil-ning [ee den-neh see-the].

1132. —— on the other side.
i den anden side.
ee den ÄN-nen see-the.

1133. —— in the middle.
i midten.
ee mid/n.

1134. Do not cut any off the top.
Lad være at klippe mit hår oppe i toppen.
lä vehr/ aw klip-peh meet hawr op-peh ee top/n.

1135. Do not cut it too short.
Klip det ikke for kort.
klip dé ig-eh for kawrt.

1136. Thin it out.   Tynd det ud.   *tḗrn dé OOTH.*

1137. (Do not) put on hair tonic.
Kom (ikke) hårvand i.
kom (ig-eh) HAWR-vän/ ee.

LAUNDRY AND DRY CLEANING
VASK OG RENSNING

**1138. Can this [laundry] deliver the clothes in one
day?**
Kan dette [vaskeri] levere tøjet på een dag?
*kä det-teh [väsk-eh-REE] lé-vé-reh TOY-eth paw ÉN
dä?*

1139. —— dry cleaner.
renseri.
rehn-seh-REE.

1140. Can I have some things washed?
Kan jeg få noget tøj vasket?
kå yĭ faw no-eth TOY väsk-eth?

1141. Will you wash and mend this shirt?
Vil De vaske og lappe denne skjorte?
vé dee väsk-eh aw lahp-peh 'den-neh SKYOHR-teh?

1142. This should not be washed in hot water.
Dette her må ikke vaskes i varmt vand.
det-teh hehr maw ig-eh väsk-es ee VAHRMT vän/.

1143. Use lukewarm water.
Brug lunkent vand.
brŏŏ lohng-kent vän/.

1144. Will you remove this stain?
Vil De tage denne plet af?
vé dee tä den-neh plet ä?

1145. (Do not) starch the collar.
Kom (ikke) stivelse i flippen.
kom (ig-eh) STEE-vel-seh ee flip/n.

1146. Will you clean and press this suit?
Vil De rense og presse denne dragt?
vé dee ren-seh aw pres-seh den-neh drahkt?

1147. There is a tear in the pocket.
Der er en rift i lommen.
dehr ehr en rift ee LOM-men.

1148. The belt is missing.
Der er intet bælte.
dehr ehr ing/n bel-teh.

1149. Will you sew on the buttons?
Vil De sy knapperne i?
vé dee sew knahp-per-neh EE?

1150. Put in a new zipper.
Sæt en ny lynlås i.
set en new lewn-laws EE.

REPAIRS
REPARATIONER

1151. My glasses are broken.
Mine briller er gået itu.
mee-neh bril/r ehr gaw-eth ee-TOO.

1152. Where can they be repaired?
Hvor kan jeg få dem repareret?
vohŕ kǎ yǐ faw dem ré-pǎ-RÉ-reth?

1153. Please regulate my watch.
Vær så venlig at regulere mit ur.
vehr saw ven-lee aw ré-gŏŏ-LÉ-reh meet OOR.

1154. My clock [loses] gains time.
Mit ur [taber] vinder.
meet OOR [tǎ-ber] vin/r.

1155. My hearing aid needs adjustment.
Mit høreapparat skal rettes.
meet HÉR-reh-ap-pa-rat/ skǎ ret-tes.

1156. I would like to have my shoes resoled.
Jeg vil gerne have mine sko forsålet.
yǐ vé gehr-neh hǎ mee-neh sko/ for-sol-leth.

1157. Will you repair [the heels]?
Vil De reparere [hælene]?
vé dee ré-pah-RÉ-reh [heh-leh-neh]?

1158. —— the strap.
remmen.
REM/en.

HEALTH AND ILLNESS
SUNDHED OG SYGDOM

1159. I wish to see [a doctor].
Jeg ønsker at se [en læge].
yĭ ẽrn-sker aw sé [en LEH-weh].

1160. —— an American doctor.
en amerikansk læge.
en ă-mé-ree-KĂNSK LEH-weh.

1161. —— a doctor who speaks English.
en læge, der taler engelsk.
en LEH-weh, dehr tă-ler EHNG-elsk.

1162. —— a specialist.
en specialist.
en spé-shă-LEEST.

1163. —— a chiropodist.
en fodlæge.
en FOHTH-leh-weh.

1164. —— an optometrist.
en optiker.
en OP-teek-er.

1165. —— an eye doctor.
en øjenlæge.
en OYN-leh-weh.

1166. Is the doctor in?
Er doktoren tilstede?
ehr DOK-teh-ren té-STEH-the?

1167. I have something in my eye.
Jeg har fået noget i øjet.
yĭ hahr faw-eth no-eth ee OY-eth.

1168. I have a headache.
Jeg har hovedpine.
yĭ hahr HOH-eth-pee-neh.

1169. I have a pain in my back.
Jeg har ondt i ryggen.
yĭ hahr OHNT ee rēg-gen.

1170. I do not sleep well.
Jeg sover ikke godt.
yĭ sow-er ig-eh got.

1171. Can you give me something to relieve my allergy?
Kan De give mig noget for min allergi?
kă dee gee mĭ no-eth for meen ăl-ler-GEE?

1172. An appendicitis attack.
En akut blindtarmsbetændelse.
en ă-KOOT blén-tahrms-bé-ten/-el-seh.

1173. An insect bite (sting).
Et insektbid (stik).
et in-SECT-beeth (stik).

1174. A blister.
En blære.
en BLAIR-eh.

1175. A boil.
En byld.
en bewl/.

1176. A burn.
En forbrænding.
en for-BREN-ning.

1177. Chills.
Kuldegysninger.
KOOL-leh-gews-ning-er.

1178. A cold.
En forkølelse.
en for-KĒR-lel-seh.

1179. Constipation.
Forstoppelse.
for-STOP-el-seh.

1180. The cough.
Hosten.
HOHS-ten.

1181. The cramp.
Krampen.
KRAHMP-en.

1182. Diarrhoea.
Diarrhé.
dee-ă-RÉ.

1183. Dysentery.
Dysenteri.
dew-sen-teh-REE.

1184. Earache.
Ørepine.
ĒR-reh-pee-neh.

1185. Fever.
Feber.
FÉ-ber.

1186. Hay fever.
Høfeber.
HĒR-fé-ber.

1187. Hoarseness.
Hæshed.
HEHS-héth.

1188. Indigestion.
Dårlig fordøjelse.
DAWR-lee for-DOY-el-seh.

1189. Nausea.
Kvalme.
kväl-meh.

1190. Pneumonia.
Lungebetændelse.
LOHNG-eh-bé-ten|-el-seh.

1191. A sore throat.
Ondt i halsen.
OHNT ee häl|-sen.

1192. A sunburn.
En solforbrænding.
en SOHL-for-bren-ning.

1193. A virus.
En virus.
en VEE-rōōs.

1194. An infection.
En infektion.
en in-fek-SHOHN.

1195. What shall I do?
Hvad skal jeg gøre?
vä skä yī GER-reh?

1196. Do I have to go to the hospital?
Er jeg nødt til at komme på hospitalet?
ehr yī NĒRT té aw kom-meh paw hoh-spee-TÄ-leth?

1197. Must I stay in bed?
Skal jeg blive i sengen?
skă yĭ blee-eh ee SENG-en?

1198. Is it contagious?
Smitter det?
smit/r dé?

1199. I feel [better] worse.
Jeg har det [bedre] dårligere.
yĭ hahr dé [beth-reh] DAWR-lee-reh.

1200. Can I travel on Monday?
Kan jeg rejse på mandag?
kă yĭ RĬ-seh paw MĂN-dä?

1201. When will you come again?
Hvornår kommer De igen?
vor-NAWR kom-mer dee ee-GEN?

1202. When shall I take [the prescription]?
Hvornår skal jeg tage [recept-medicinen]?
vor-NAWR skă yĭ tä [ré-SEPT-mé-dee-see-nen]?

1203. —— the medicine.
medicinen.
mé-dee-SEE-nen.

1204. —— the pills.
pillerne.
pil-ler-neh.

1205. Every hour.
Hver time.
VEHR tee-meh.

1206. Before [after] meals.
Før [efter] måltiderne.
FĔRR/ [eft/r] MOL-tee-ther-neh.

1207. When I go to bed.
Når jeg går i seng.
nawr yǐ gawr ee-SENG.

1208. When I get up.
Når jeg står op.
nawr yǐ stawr OP.

1209. Twice a day.
To gange dagligt.
TOH gahng-eh DAH-lee.

1210. A drop.
En dråbe.
en DRAW-beh.

1211. A teaspoonful.
En teskefuld.
en TÉ-ské-fōōl/.

1212. X-rays.
Røntgenstraaler.
RĒRNT-gen-straw-ler.

ACCIDENTS

ULYKKESTILFÆLDE

1213. Will you get [a doctor].
Vil De få fat på [en læge].
vé dee faw fat paw [en LEH-weh].

1214. —— a nurse.
en sygeplejerske.
en SEW-eh-plǐ-er-skeh.

1215. —— an ambulance.
en ambulance.
en ăm-bōō-LAHNG-seh.

1216. He has [fallen] fainted.
Han er [faldet] besvimet.
han ehr [fål-leth] bé-SVEE-meth.

1217. She has cut herself.
Hun har skåret sig.
hōōn hahr skaw-reth sī.

1218. She has sprained her wrist.
Hun har forstuvet håndleddet.
hoon hahr for-stoo-veth HON-léth-eth.

1219. She has [a bruise].
Hun har fået [en kvæstelse].
hōōn hahr faw-eth [en KVES-tel-seh].

1220. —— a fracture.
et brud.
et brōōth.

1221. Can you dress this wound?
Kan De forbinde dette sår?
kå dee for-bin-neh det-teh sawr/?

1222. It [is bleeding] is swollen.
Det [bløder] er opsvulmet.
dé [BLĒR-ther] ehr OP-svōōl-meth.

1223. I need something for a tourniquet.
Jeg har brug for noget til en årepresse.
yĩ hahr brōō for no-eth té en AW-reh-pres-seh.

1224. Are you all right?
Er De all right?
ehr dee "all right"?

1225. I have hurt my foot.
Jeg har stødt min fod.
yĩ hahr stērt meen fohth.

1226. I want to rest for a moment.
Jeg må hvile et øjeblik.
yĭ maw vee-leh et OY-eh-blik.

1227. Will you notify [my husband]?
Vil De give [min mand] besked?
vé dee gee [meen măn/] bé-skéth?

1228. —— my wife.
min kone.
meen koh-neh.

PARTS OF THE BODY
LEGEMSDELE

1229. The appendix. Blindtarmen. *BLIN-tahr-men.*

1230. The arm. Armen. *ahr-men.*

1231. The artery. Pulsåren. *pŏŏls-aw-ren.*

1232. The back. Ryggen. *rēg-gen.*

1233. The blood. Blodet. *bloh/-thet.*

1234. The blood vessels. Blodkarrene. *BLOHTH-kahr-neh*

1235. The bone. Knoglen. *k-now-len.*

1236. The brain. Hjernen. *yehr-nen.*

1237. The breast. Brystet. *brēr-steth.*

1238. The cheek. Kinden. *KIN/-nen.*

1239. The chest. Brystet. *brēr-steth.*

1240. The chin. Hagen. *HÄ-wen.*

1241. The collarbone. Kravebenet. *krah-veh-bé-neth.*

1242. The ear. Øret. *ĒR-reth.*

1243. The elbow. Albuen. *ÄL-bŏŏ-en.*

1244. The eye. Øjet. *OY-eth.*

1245. The eyebrows. Øjenbrynene. *OYN-brew-neh-neh.*

1246. The eyelashes. Øjenvipperne. *OYN-vépr-neh.*

1247. The eyelid. Øjenlåget. *OYN-law-weth.*

1248. The face. Ansigtet. *ÄN-sik-teth.*

1249. The finger. Fingeren. *FING/-eh-ren.*

1250. The fingernail. Neglen. *NĪ/-len.*

1251. The foot. Foden. *FOH-then.*

1252. The forehead. Panden. *PÄN-nen.*

1253. The gall bladder. Galdeblæren. *GÄL-leh-bleh-ren.*

1254. The glands. Kirtlerne. *KEERT-ler-neh.*

1255. The gums. Gummerne. *GOHM-mer-neh.*

1256. The hair. Håret. *HAW/-reth.*

1257. The head. Hovedet. *HOH-thet.*

1258. The hand. Hånden. *HON/-nen.*

1259. The heart. Hjertet. *YEHR-teth.*

1260. The heel. Hælen. *HEH/-len.*

1261. The hip. Hoften. *HOF-ten.*

1262. The intestines. Tarmene. *TAHR-meh-neh.*

1263. The jaw. Kæben. *KEH-ben.*

1264. The joint. Leddet. *LÉTH-thet.*

1265. The kidney. Nyren. *NEW-ren.*

1266. The knee. Knæet. *K-NEH-eth.*

1267. The leg. Benet. *BÉ-neth.*

1268. The lip. Læben. *LEH-ben.*

1269. The liver. Leveren. *LÉ-veh-ren.*

1270. The lungs. Lungerne. *LOHNG-er-neh.*

1271. The mouth. Munden. *MOHN/-nen.*

1272. The muscle. Muskelen. *MOOSK-len.*

1273. The neck. Nakken. *NÄK-n.*

1274. The nerve. Nerven. *NEHR-ven.*

1275. The nose. Næsen. *NEH-sen.*

1276. The rib. Ribbenet. *REE-bé-neth.*

1277. The shoulder. Skulderen. *SKOOL-ren.*

1278. The skin. Huden. *HOO-then.*

1279. The skull. Hjerneskallen. *YEHR-neh-skäl/n.*

1280. The spine. Rygraden. *RĒRG-räh-then.*

1281. The stomach. Maven. *MÄ-ven.*

1282. The throat.   Halsen.   *HÅL-sen.*

1283. The toe, toes.   Tåen, tæerne.   *TAW/n, TEH-er-neh.*

1284. The toenail.   Tånegl.   *taw-ni̇l.*

1285. The tongue.   Tungen.   *TOHNG-en.*

1286. The tonsils.   Mandlerne.   *MÄN-ler-neh.*

1287. The tooth, teeth.   Tanden, tænderne.
    TÄN-nen, TEN-ner-neh.

1288. The vein.   Åren.   *aw-ren.*

DENTIST

TANDLÆGE

1289. Do you know a good dentist?
    Kender De en god tandlæge?
    ken-ner dee en goh TÄN-leh-weh?

1290. I have pain in this wisdom tooth.
    Jeg har ondt i den visdomstand.
    yi̇ hahr ohnt ee den/ vees-doms-tän.

1291. I have lost a filling.
    Jeg har tabt en plombe.
    yi̇ hahr täbt en plohm-beh.

1292. I'm afraid that I have an abscess.
    Jeg er bange for jeg har en byld.
    yi̇ ehr bahng-eh for yi̇ hahr en BEWL/.

1293. I have broken a tooth.
    Jeg har brækket en tand.
    yi̇ har brek-keth en tän/.

1294. Can you fix [the bridge] temporarily?
    Kan De ordne [broen] foreløbigt?
    ka dee ord-neh [BROH-en] FAW-reh-lēr-bee?

1295. ——— the denture.
    protesen.
    proh-TÉ-sen.

1296. This hurts.
    Det gør ondt.
    dé gḗrr OHNT/.

1297. Will you give me [a local anesthetic].
    Vil De give mig [en lokalbedøvelse].
    vé dee gee mĭ [en lo-KĂL/-bé-dḗr-vel-seh].

1298. ——— gas.
    en gasbedøvelse.
    en GĂS/-bé-dḗr-vel-seh.

USEFUL INFORMATION
PRAKTISKE OPLYSNINGER

TIME
TIDEN, KLOKKEN

1299. What time is it?
    Hvad er klokken?
    vă ehr klok/n?

1300. It is [early].
    Klokken er [ikke ret mange].
    klok/n ehr [ig-eh ret mahng-eh].

1301. ——— late.
    mange.
    mahng-eh.

1302. Now it is too late.
    Nu er det for sent.
    noo ehr dé for sént.

1303. It is 1 A.M.
　　Klokken er 1 (eet).*
　　klok/n ehr ÉT.

1304. It is [two o'clock A.M.].
　　Klokken er [2 (to)].
　　klok/n ehr [TOH/].

1305. —— half-past three P.M.
　　　　15.30 (femten-tredive).
　　　　fem-ten trehth-veh.

1306. —— a quarter past four P.M.
　　　　16.15 (seksten-femten) (et kvarter over 16).
　　　　sĭ-sten-fem-ten (et kvahr-tér ow/r sĭ-sten).

1307. —— a quarter to five P.M.
　　　　et kvarter i 17 (sytten).
　　　　et kvahr-tér ee sērt-ten.

1308. At ten minutes to six A.M.
　　Klokken ti minutter i 6 (seks).
　　klok/n tee mee-noodr ee sex.

1309. At twenty minutes past seven P.M.
　　Klokken tyve minutter over 19 (nitten).
　　klok/n tew-veh mee-noodr ow/r nét-ten.

1310. In the morning.
　　Om morgenen.
　　om MOR-nen.

1311. In the forenoon.
　　Om formiddagen.
　　om FOR-meh-dä-en.

1312. In the afternoon.
　　Om eftermiddagen
　　om EFT/r-mé-dä-en.

* In Denmark the A.M. and P.M. expressions are not used.
One to twelve P.M. are therefore expressed in numbers from
thirteen to twenty-four.

1313. In the evening.
Om aftenen.
om AHFT-nen.

1314. At noon.
Klokken 12 middag.
klok/n tol/ MÉ-dä.

1315. The day.
Dagen.
dä-en.

1316. The night.
Natten.
nät/n.

1317. Day and night (24 hours).
Et døgn.   (Danish word for 24 hrs.).
et doyn.

1318. Midnight.
Midnat.   (KL.24)
MEETH-nät.   (klok/n feer-aw-tew-veh)

1319. Last night.
I går nat.
ee gawr NÄT.

1320. Yesterday.
I går.
ee GAWR.

1321. Today.
I dag.
ee DÄ/.

1322. Tonight.
I aften.
ee AHFT/n.

1323. Tomorrow.
I morgen.
ee MAW-ren.

1324. Last month.
Sidste måned.
sees-teh MAW-neth.

1325. Last year.
Sidste år.
sees-teh AWR.

1326 Next Sunday
Næste søndag.
nes-teh SERN-dä.

1327. Next week.
Næste uge.
nes-teh OO-eh.

1328. The day before yesterday.
I forgårs.
ee FOR-gawrs.

1329. The day after tomorrow.
I overmorgen.
ee OW/r-maw-ren.

1330. Two weeks ago.
For to uger siden.
for toh OO-er see-then.

WEATHER

VEJRET

1331. How is the weather today?
Hvordan er vejret idag?
VOH-den ehr veh-reth ee-DÄ?

1332. Is it cold?
Er det koldt?
ehr dé KOL/t?

1333. Is it fair?
Er det godt?
ehr dé GOT?

1334. Is it hot?
Er det varmt?
ehr dé vahrmt?

1335. Is it raining?
Regner det?
RI-ner dé?

1336. Is it snowing?
    Sner det?
    snér dé?

1337. Is it sunny?
    Skinner solen?
    SKIN/r SOH-len?

1338. Is it very warm?
    Er det meget varmt?
    ehr dé mī-eth vahrmt?

1339. I want to sit [in the shade].
    Jeg vil sidde [i skyggen].
    yī vé séth-the [ee skewg-gen].

1340. —— in the sun.
    i solen.
    ee SOH-len.

DAYS OF THE WEEK
UGENS DAGE

1341. Monday. Mandag. *MÄN-dä.*
1342. Tuesday. Tirsdag. *TEERS-dä.*
1343. Wednesday. Onsdag. *OHNS-dä.*
1344. Thursday. Torsdag. *TAWRS-dä.*
1345. Friday. Fredag. *FRÉ-dä.*
1346. Saturday. Lørdag. *LĒRR-dä.*
1347. Sunday. Søndag. *SĒRN-dä.*

MONTHS AND SEASONS
MÅNEDER OG ÅRSTIDER

1348. January. Januar. *YÄ-nŏŏ-ahr.*
1349. February. Februar. *FÉB-rŏŏ-ahr.*

1350. **March.** Marts. *mahrts.*

1351. **April.** April. *ǎ-PREEL.*

1352. **May.** Maj. *mǐ/.*

1353. **June.** Juni. *YOO-nee.*

1354. **July.** Juli. *YOO-lee.*

1355. **August.** August. *ow-GOHST/.*

1356. **September.** September. *sép-TEM-ber.*

1357. **October.** Oktober. *ohk-TOH-ber.*

1358. **November.** November. *no-VEM-ber.*

1359. **December.** December. *dé-SEM-ber.*

1360. **Spring.** Forår. *FOR-awr.*

1361. **Summer.** Sommer. *SOM/r.*

1362. **Autumn.** Efterår. *EFT/r-awr.*

1363. **Winter.** Vinter. *VIN-ter.*

HOLIDAYS AND GREETINGS
HELLIGDAGE OG HILSENER

1364. **Christmas.** Jul. *YOOL/.*

1365. **Easter.** Påske. *PAW-skeh.*

1366. **Good Friday.** Langfredag. *lahng-FRÉ-dǎ.*

1367. **Shrovetide.*** Fastelavn. *fǎs-teh-LOWN.*

1368. **New Year's Day.** Nytårsdag. *newt-awrs-dǎ.*

1369. **Legal holidays.**
Lovbefalede fridage.
low-bé-fǎ-leh-the FREE-dǎ-eh.

1370. **Happy Birthday!**
Tillykke med fødselsdagen!
té-lērk-keh meh FĒR-sels-dǎ-en!

* As Denmark is a Protestant country there is no fasting during Lent but feasting at Shrovetide.

1371. Happy New Year!
Godt Nytår!
GOT newt-awr!

1372. Merry Christmas!
Glædelig Jul!
GLEH-the-lee YOOL|!

NUMBERS : CARDINAL
TAL: GRUNDTAL

1373. 0. **Zero.** Nul. *nohl.*

1. **One.** Een, eet. (*én, ét.*)

2. **Two.** To. *toh|.*

3. **Three.** Tre. *tré|.*

4. **Four.** Fire. *fee-reh.*

5. **Five.** Fem. *fem|.*

6. **Six.** Seks. *sex.*

7. **Seven.** Syv. *sewv|.*

8. **Eight.** Otte. *aw-teh.*

9. **Nine.** Ni. *nee|.*

10. **Ten.** Ti. *tee|.*

11. **Eleven.** Elleve. *el-veh.*

12. **Twelve.** Tolv. *tol|.*

13. **Thirteen.** Tretten. *tret-ten.*

14. **Fourteen.** Fjorten. *fyohr-ten.*

15. **Fifteen.** Femten. *fem-ten.*

16. **Sixteen.** Seksten. *sĭ-sten.*

17. **Seventeen.** Sytten. *sẽrt-ten.*

18. **Eighteen.** Atten. *aht-ten.*

19. **Nineteen.** Nitten. *nét-ten.*

20. **Twenty.** Tyve. *tew-veh.*

21. **Twenty-one.** En-og-tyve. *én-aw-tew-veh.*

22. **Twenty-two.** To-og-tyve. *toh-aw-tew-veh.*

30. **Thirty.** Tredive. *treth-veh.*

31. **Thirty-one.** En-og-tredive. *én-aw-treth-veh.*

40. **Forty.** Fyrre. *fẽrr-reh.*

50. **Fifty.** Halvtreds. *hăl-trés.*

60. **Sixty.** Tres. *trés.*

70. **Seventy.** Halvfjerds. *hăl-fyehrs.*

71. **Seventy-one.** Een og halvfjerds. *én-aw-hăl-fyehrs.*

80. **Eighty.** Firs. *feers.*

81. **Eighty-one.** Een og firs. *én-aw-feers.*

90. **Ninety.** Halvfems. *hăl-fems.*

91. **Ninety-one.** Een og halvfems. *én-aw-hăl-fems.*

100. **One hundred.** Hundrede. *hoon-reh-the.*

200. **Two hundred.** To hundrede. *TOH-hoon-reh-the.*

1000. **One thousand.** Tusind. *too-sen.*

2000. **Two thousand.** To tusind. *TOH-too-sen.*

1374. Today is November 5, 1957.

Idag er det den 5. November 1957.

ee-dă ehr dé den fem-teh NO-vem-ber, nét-ten hŏŏn-reh-the aw sewv aw hăl-trés.

1375. Your letter of today's date.

Deres brev af dags dato.

deh-res brév ă dăs dă-to.

NUMBERS : ORDINALS
TAL: ORDENSTAL

1376. First. Første. *fẽrr-steh.*
Second. Anden. *ăn-nen.*
Third. Tredie. *tréth-yeh.*

Fourth. Fjerde. *fyeh-reh.*

Fifth. Femte. *fem-teh.*

Sixth. Sjette. *sheh-teh.*

Seventh. Syvende. *sew-veh-neh.*

Eighth. Ottende. *awt-teh-neh.*

Ninth. Niende. *nee-en-neh.*

Tenth. Tiende. *tee-en-neh.*

COMMON ARTICLES
ALMINDELIGE BRUGSTING

1377. The ash tray.
Askebægeret.
ÄS-keh-beh-ret.

1378. The basket.
Kurven.
köör-ven.

1379. The bobby pins.
Hårklemmerne.
hawr-klemr-neh.

1380. The bottle opener
Flaskeåbneren.
FLÄS-keh-awb-neh-ren.

1381. The box.
Æsken.
ES-ken.

1382. The bracelet.
Armbåndet.
AHRM-bon/-neth.

1383. The brooch.
Broschen.
braw-shen.

1384. The bulb (light).
Den elektriske pære.
den é-LEK-tree-skeh PEH-reh.

1385. The candy.
Chokoladen (konfekten).
shoh-ko-LÅ-then (kohn-fek-ten).

1386. The hard candy.
Bolsjerne.
bawl-sher-neh.

1387. The can opener.
Dåseoplukkeren.
DAW-seh-op-lohk-ren.

1388. Canvas (artist's).
Lærred.
LEHR-reth.

1389. The china.
Porcelænet.
por-sé-LEH-neth.

1390. The cloth.
Klædet.
KLEH-thet.

1391. The clock.
Uret.
OO-reth.

1392. The compact.
Kompakten.
kom-påk-ten.

1393. The cork.
Proppen.
PROP/n.

1394. The corkscrew.
Proptrækkeren.
PROP-trek/ren.

1395. Cotton.
Bomulden.
BOM-ööl-len.

1396. The cuff links.
Manchetknapperne.
mahng-SHET-knapr-neh.

1397. The cushion.
Puden.
POO-then.

1398. The doll.
Dukken.
DOHK/n.

1399. The earrings.
Øreringene.
ĒR-reh-ring-eh-neh.

1400. The embroidery.
Broderiet.
broh-dé-REE-eth.

1401. The flashlight.
Lommelygten.
LOM-meh-lērk-ten.

1402. The gum (chewing).
Tyggegummiet.
TEWG-geh-goh-mee-eth.

1403. The handbag.
Håndtasken.
HON-täs-ken.

1404. The hairnet.
Hårnettet.
HAWR-net-eth.

1405. The iron (flat).
Strygejernet.
STREW-eh-yehr-neth.

1406. The jewelry (gold, silver).
Smykkerne (guld, sølv).
SMERK-er-neh (gōōl, sērl).

1407. The lace (hand-made).
Kniplingen.
knip-ling-en.

1408. The lace (machine-made).
Blonderne.
blon-der-neh.

1409. The leather.
Læderet.
LEH-the-reth.

1410. The linen.
Lærredet.
LEHR-reh-thet.

1411. The mirror.
Spejlet.
SPI/-leth.

1412. The sheet music.
Nodeheftet.
no-the-hef-tet.

1413. The musical instruments.
Musikinstrumenterne.
möö-SEEK-in-stroo-ment-er-neh.

1414. The nail file.
Neglefilen.
NĪ-leh-fee-len.

1415. The necklace.
Halsbåndet.
HAHLS-bon/-neth.

1416. The needle.
Nålen.
NAW-len.

1417. The notebook.
Lommebogen.
LOM-meh-baw-wen.

1418. The oil painting.
Oliemaleriet.
OHL-yeh-mä-leh-REE-eth.

1419. The pail.
Spanden.
SPÄN/en.

1420. The penknife.
Lommekniven.
LOM-mek-nee-ven.

1421. The perfume.
Parfumen.
pahr-FEW-men.

1422. The pin (straight).
Knappenålen.
k-nap-peh-naw-len.

1423. The radio.
Radioen.
RAH-dee-ohn.

1424. The records (discs).
Grammofonpladerne.
grahm-må-FOHN-plä-ther-neh.

1425. The ring.
Ringen.
RING/-en.

1426. The rubbers.
Galoscherne.
gå-LOS-sher-neh.

1427. The rug.
Tæppet.
TEP-eth.

1428. The safety pin.
Sikkerhedsnålen.
SIK/r-héths-naw-len.

1429. The scissors.
Saksen.
SAHK-sen.

1430. The screw.
Skruen.
SKROO-en.

1431. The silk.
Silken.
silk-en.

1432. The silverware.
Sølvtøjet.
SERL-toy-eth.

1433. The stone (precious).
Ædelstenen.
EH-thel-sté-nen.

1434. The stopper.
Proppen.
PROP/n.

1435. The straw.
Strået.
STRAW/-eth.

1436. The tablecloth.
Dugen.
DOO-wen.

!437. The thimble.
Fingerbøllet.
FING-er-bĕri-leth.

1438. The thread.
Tråden.
TRAW-then.

!439. The toys.
Legetøjet.
LI-eh-toy-eth.

1440. The umbrella.
Paraplyen.
pä-rä-PLEW-en.

1441. The vase.
Vasen.
VÄ-sen.

1442. The whiskbroom (clothes-brush).
Klædebørsten.
KLEH-the-bĕrr-sten.

1443. The wire.
Ståltråd.
STOL-trawth.

1444. The wood.
Træet.
TREH-eth.

1445. The wool.
Ulden.
OOL/n.

INDEX

Please note: Capitalized items in the index refer to section headings, and the references immediately following (labeled p.) refer to page numbers; all other numbers refer to specific entries, which are numbered consecutively from 1 to 1445.

153